Worth the Risk

Discovering God's purpose for my
dreams as a baseball agent.

DAVID PASTI

Ark House Press
arkhousepress.com

© 2025 David Pasti

All rights reserved. Apart from any fair dealing for the purpose of study, research, criticism, or review, as permitted under the Copyright Act, no part may be reproduced by any process without written permission.

Cataloguing in Publication Data:
Title: Worth the Risk
ISBN: 978-1-7641362-2-8 (pbk)
Subjects: [BIO016000] BIOGRAPHY & AUTOBIOGRAPHY / Sports; [REL012170] RELIGION / Christian Living / Personal Memoirs; [REL012040]   RELIGION / Christian Living / Inspirational.

Edited by Danielle Ripley Burgess
Design by initiateagency.com

"As is the case for many of us the path to success and meaning is often not a straight line, but a wild and confusing route filled with highs and lows. David takes us on his winding road in *Worth the Risk*, a journey that will inspire and encourage as we navigate our own path. He was an instrumental figure in my own journey as an 18 year old playing Minor League Baseball. I am still grateful for his help all those years ago and now grateful to experience this story."

Joel Klatt - Fox Sports Lead CFB analyst…
Former Minor League client

"Dave Pasti is a man of remarkable faith and profound resilience. In *Worth The Risk*, he weaves a gripping account of his years as a baseball agent and his pursuit of God's purpose for his life. Deeply honest and rich with humanity and humility, *Worth The Risk* is well worth your time."

Wayne Coffey is the author of more than 30 books, including five New York Times bestsellers.

His chronicle of the 1980 U.S. Olympic hockey team, *The Boys of Winter*, is widely regarded as the best book ever written on the so-called "Miracle On Ice."

"Dave Pasti introduced himself to me as a "new agent" at the MLB Winter Meetings in 2002. As a "veteran agent" at that point, similar introductions had happened to me over the years, and I always hoped those I'd met would turn out to be good, honest, ethical additions to the agent business. Unfortunately, that didn't always prove to be the case! Dave proved over the years to be an exception to those kind of exposures. He was always an honest, caring, highly-ethical and hard-working individual, always going the extra mile to do the right thing for his clients. I looked forward to seeing him at numerous events over the years, and enjoyed hearing his play-by-play of his positive progress and successes in our business."

Joe Bick – MLB Agent – Meister Sports Management

"David embarks on a transformative journey of faith as he faces the challenges of pursuing his dreams, regardless of the risks involved. Through the trials and triumphs, he discovers that true leadership and success stem not only from ambition but also from love, purpose, and a surrender to God's presence and power. His experiences in the world of sports and law highlight the importance of balancing personal aspirations with family and faith, ultimately leading him to a fulfilling life beyond the diamond. "

Dan Britton, President/CEO of SportsLife and bestselling author of One Word and Daily Wisdom for Men.

Contents

Foreword 1
Chapter 1:   Regrets 5
Chapter 2:   Sense of Adventure 10
Chapter 3:   Finding Myself 17
Chapter 4:   A New Creation 23
Chapter 5:   Starting a Family and a Law Practice 29
Chapter 6:   Searching for Significance 36
Chapter 7:   Taking the Plunge 44
Chapter 8:   The Annual Baseball Draft 48
Chapter 9:   Finally: A Prospect 54
Chapter 10: The Long Shot 59
Chapter 11: Balancing Act 65
Chapter 12: Aaron Laffey 70
Chapter 13: Minor League Agent 78
Chapter 14: Hitting Bottom 85
Chapter 15: Finally: A Major League Rep 93
Chapter 16: The Offseason 105

Chapter 17: Time for Investors 111

Chapter 18: Fish or Cut Bait 124

Chapter 19: Arbitration 134

Chapter 20: Letting Go 140

Chapter 21: Not All It's Cracked Up To Be 148

Chapter 22: Living with Purpose 157

Dedication 163

Acknowledgements 165

Foreword

Jackie Robinson once stated, "A life is not important except in the impact it has on other lives." This is a pertinent quote to keep in mind as you read through the pages of my good friend Dave Pasti's journey to becoming a successful Major League Baseball Player Agent. I had the very good fortune to observe much of what Dave recounts here, as I was privileged for many years to be Dave's partner in our agency, Diakon Baseball Group. Not long after we both retired from representing players, Dave continued to use his formidable legal skills to practice law, and help those less fortunate through Christian Legal Aid and, as I was an ordained Anglican priest, he sent me a spreadsheet tallying up our combined careers. We represented nearly 70 players in the Major League Baseball draft and another nine players who reached the Major Leagues. While those quantitative numbers might seem impressive, it is just here where I will refer the reader back to the above Jackie Robinson quote, and why it applies to Dave Pasti.

Everyone thinks being a sports' agent is like what's portrayed in the movie 'Jerry Maguire,' with Tom Cruise. The reality is that it's much less glamorous. There is a 95 percent failure rate for those who think they have what it takes to be a sports agent. For a baseball agent, the quality of one's clients determines their career path. Dave and I each learned early on there was a big difference between 'prospects,' players who had a legitimate chance to become Major Leaguers, and 'suspects,' those who would survive in the minor leagues for a few years before joining the rest of us in the working world. Most agents look at their clients as a means to an end – the end being the four percent commission they earn on a draft bonus or Major League salary. But this was not how Dave Pasti viewed his clients. Dave viewed his clients as people first, as sons and husbands second, and as baseball players third. I was a witness to countless conversations Dave had with his clients regarding the myriad of issues that confront aspiring professional baseball players – slumps, injuries, girlfriends/wives, a family crisis, miserly teams, and Dave always provided calming, honest, wise counsel, with a reassuring and steady hand. This is the wonderful impact that Dave had on other people's lives. You will see in the following pages that Dave's Christian faith is foundational to his life, and the impact he had on his players was always rooted in his sincere faith.

During the time period Dave writes about in these pages, I can also assure you Dave's impact on other people's lives extended beyond just his players. Like concentric circles going outward, scouts, coaches, front office personnel, player's parents, and even representatives from Nike, Reebok, and Topps Baseball Cards, among others, were at one point all impacted for the good by Dave's competent yet caring demeanor. When the hard aggressive work of a negotiation was done, Dave always saw the other side as a human being. You will also see, in the following pages, the impact Dave had on the people most important to him, his wife Marie, and three sons, as a faithful and devoted husband and father.

I would be remiss if I didn't include the impact Dave had on my own life. I used to tell Dave frequently that he was always the better lawyer of the two of us. Sometimes I would be searching for something in Major League Baseball's Collective Bargaining Agreement, or the NCAA Manual, (both documents being as accessible and understandable as the US tax code) and I would make a quick call to Dave, and he would almost instantly direct me

FOREWORD

to the appropriate provision. Having Dave as my partner certainly made me better as a baseball agent but, more importantly, a better person. There were no short cuts or grey areas with Dave, always and only integrity, and our shared faith. I can honestly and truly say that Dave Pasti is one of the very few people whom I would, without reservation, place my life in his hands.

Lastly, I am quite certain that when you finish reading Dave's inspiring and heartfelt story, you will also be able to add your own name to the list of people whose life Dave Pasti has impacted.

Rev. Joseph A. Kohm, Jr.
April, 2025
Virginia Beach, Va.

CHAPTER 1

Regrets

Therefore do not worry about tomorrow, for tomorrow will worry about itself. Each day has enough trouble of its own.

MATTHEW 6:34

On December 29, 1995, the course of my life changed forever.

It started out as a normal Friday. I was in the process of moving my law office in Rockville, a suburb of Washington DC. I had opened my own law practice just three years earlier, and its success meant I was already moving to another location near the courthouse. I spent most of the day with the telecommunications guy as he hooked up the phones. My wife, Marie, was with our two toddlers, Jonathan and Michael, and had left for her parent's house in Alexandria for the night, trying to avoid DC's afternoon rush-hour traffic. I had my usual Friday night dinner plans with Dad, who had moved in with us six months earlier. For four years, he'd been living with amyloidosis, a rare blood disorder that creates too many white blood cells that attach themselves to various organs in the body. For

Dad, the disease affected his kidneys. We had been renting a house in Falls Church, Virginia, another suburb of Washington DC, and we were already thinking of buying a home near Rockville when my father reached a point where he could no longer live alone. We prayed about how to help, and it became clear him living with us was the right thing to do.

We found a home that accommodated him and, in April, we moved in. My dad came in June.

But ever since Christmas Day, I had grown increasingly concerned about my father's health. I had watched him get a stent put in his arm to prepare him for dialysis in November. But one month later, his coughing had increased, and he stayed in the basement most of the day. I called my siblings, and my older sister, Sara, recommended I call his treating doctor. I spoke with the doctor, and he suggested Dad go in and see him after the first of the year.

I was focused on moving into my new law office at the start of the new year, but I was still making time to journal. It was something I'd committed to for years. On the morning of December 29, I sat down to write in my journal.

12/29/95

Anxiety not just from change, but status, new office gives the appearance that I know what I'm doing. But it's good to grow as long as I don't get ahead of myself.

When I got home, Dad was sitting quietly at the dining room table waiting for me to take him out to eat. We drove a short distance to Red Lobster, one of his favorite places. We went to the restaurant in silence.

Once seated, I was surprised Dad ordered a Mai Tai. He usually didn't drink. But his drink order would soon make sense.

During dinner, Dad seemed slower in his movements and speech, and he seemed depressed. Without any questioning, and with his head down, he began to share some of his deepest thoughts.

> Dad: "I never had anyone to talk to. Everyone is too busy."
> Me: "Are you open to counseling?"
> Dad: "I don't know" (as he took another sip of his Mai Tai).

He began to share his soul, talking about his regrets. I knew what he meant, because although he talked with everyone he met, he didn't have anyone to share his innermost thoughts with anymore. My mother had been stricken with multiple sclerosis (MS) in her thirties. Mom's severe case of MS affected her both physically and mentally. It took a toll on everyone in our family, especially Dad. My two older siblings, who are five and seven years older than me, knew my mom when she was well. My younger sister and I only have a few memories of a healthy mom.

Mom's illness also affected my dad's career. He lost his ability to be flexible. He worked a steady job at IBM all throughout my childhood, but it left him unfulfilled. As a boy, I overheard him complain about his job several times.

During our dinner conversation (and maybe thanks to his Mai Tai), he began opening up and looking back on his career, sharing about how he felt he had no choice. He couldn't leave a job he hated while his wife was ill, and he had four kids to raise. Although I had become more and more aware of his sacrifice as I'd begun my own career and family, I wondered why he was telling me this nine years after he retired.

Our server put the bill on the table, and I looked to my dad. He always insisted on paying. But he was having a difficult time signing his name on the credit card receipt. Afterward, he struggled to get out of his seat and, unlike any other time, I had to help him with his jacket. He walked very slowly to the front of the restaurant. I wasn't sure if he was just depressed, or if there was something more serious going on with his health. Either way, I was very concerned.

On the drive back home, like the drive to the restaurant, there was complete silence. I kept thinking I needed to stay with him when we got home. I parked the car in the driveway and my dad walked slowly toward the house. I was following right behind. As we entered the house, my dad fell backwards. I caught his fall. He was still breathing, but he didn't say anything. He was in my arms, and I sat with him for about 20 seconds. Then I heard a wheezing sound for five to ten seconds. I started to give him mouth to mouth, and felt a pulse. I ran to the phone and couldn't get a dial tone. I found another phone and called 911, but got cut off. Panic set in. I was yelling "Please don't die!" Finally, I got through to 911 and they calmed me down. The paramedics were at my house within a few minutes. They said he still had a pulse, which gave me hope. But I began to cry as the reality of what was happening set in. I thought about my dad not being alive to enjoy his grandkids, and to watch them grow up.

The police arrived and escorted me to the hospital, following the ambulance that carried Dad. It wasn't long before the doctor found me in the hospital waiting room and told me Dad had died of congestive heart failure. He was 73 years old. In shock, I called my wife and siblings. My wife immediately got into the car, and drove from her parent's house to the hospital. My younger sister came as soon as she could to join us there. (My older siblings lived out of the area.)

I wasn't prepared to lose him. I was overwhelmed with sadness. I was also traumatized. I had never watched anyone die. I kept thinking, *At least I had one last conversation with him, and he didn't die alone.*

Over the next few months, I continued to process his death. Was there anything I could have done? Should I have taken him to the hospital after dinner? It didn't take long for me to realize there was nothing I could have done, or could do differently. In fact, I came to realize Dad knew he was going to die. In his room, we found an obituary he had prepared for us just three weeks prior to his death.

For the next year, I was in a fog. I began to look at my life, and where I was going. I had lost my mother at age 20 in 1981 and now, in 1995 at age 35, I had lost both of my parents. Perhaps I was going through a midlife crisis. I had eagerly read a book called *Listening to Midlife*, looking for answers. The author indicated that people who lose both of their parents tend to go through a midlife crisis earlier than others. I began to ask myself hard questions.

Sure, sometimes I felt a little burned out with the daily grind of paying the bills, and I didn't necessarily see myself practicing criminal defense law for the rest of my life. But I felt satisfied for the most part. I enjoyed helping people. My law practice was getting off the ground, and we were going in the right direction with our family. My wife could stay home with our two young boys, as she had hoped, and we were generally happy.

But I kept going back to how depressed Dad was just before he died. And I began to ask myself, *What do I want my life to look like when reach the end? Will I regret any roads not taken?*

My hard questions led to answers that surprised me.

CHAPTER 2

Sense of Adventure

> Life is either a great adventure or it's nothing.
> HELEN KELLER

I always had a sense of adventure. I'm sure I got it from Dad. As my uncle would tell me after Dad passed, he was full of adventure as a boy and young man. Dad grew up in Chicago, about a mile from Wrigley Field. He was the son of Romanian immigrants who came through Ellis Island in search of the American dream. He grew up playing baseball and rooting for the Cubs. I remember Dad telling me about going to the World Series to see Babe Ruth in 1935 and 1938. He used to swim in Lake Michigan almost every day in the summer. One day, when he was 17, he took a 150-mile round trip bike ride to Lake Geneva with a friend. That's pretty good for a bike with only one gear!

Dad graduated high school in 1940. He was captain of the basketball team and class president. He then attended Northwestern University for three years before enlisting in the Army Air Corp in 1943. He was stationed in China during WWII. Upon returning to the States, he went out to Wyoming to work on a ranch for six weeks during two summers. He finished school and became a high school math teacher and basketball coach in Minnesota. He was full of life.

Dad met Mom while he was in graduate school. My mother was from an upper middle-class family from Paw Paw, Michigan. Her father owned a car dealership. Dad and Mom married the same year they met, and they began having children within their first year of marriage. Prompted by my mom's feeling that they needed more money, Dad left teaching and coaching to work in sales for IBM when he was 35 years old.

Mom and Dad, December 1952

Early in my childhood, we moved several times due to Dad's job. I was born in Peoria, Illinois, in 1960. From there, I lived in Glen Ellyn, Illinois, from 1962 to 1965, and then Poughkeepsie, New York, from 1965 to 1968. Our last move was to Rockville, Maryland, in 1968, where I lived until I graduated from high school. I was young for most of our moves, and it was exciting to live in new places. Because of my athletic abilities, I was always involved in sports, and found it was easy to make new friends.

Years later, I found out Dad had a choice between moving to San Jose, California, or the Washington DC area, and he chose Washington DC because it offered more access to medical care. Unbeknownst to me, my mom had already been diagnosed with MS while we were living in New York. My first memory of seeing her with symptoms was when she took me to the store, and one of the employees asked me what was wrong with my mother. At nine years old, I had learned she had MS, and that's what I told the clerk.

Soon enough, my mom's symptoms became worse. That trip to the store would be one of the last times she drove. Her thinking became much more irrational. She would take a cab to the store and buy Wink and Doritos, even though we had several bottles of Wink, and numerous bags of Doritos, at home. She mainly stayed home and watched TV, but she also read her Bible a lot.

Mom's disease drained the life out of Dad. Our family was unable to reason with her. Dad got more and more upset about his job as coworkers, much younger than him, got promoted. His supervisor was more than ten years younger than him, and it was clear he wasn't happy about it. He had a short fuse, and was easily angered. Most evenings, my dad would sit in the living room reading, while my mom would be in the family room watching TV. There would be occasional yelling going back and forth, mostly my father raising his voice and telling my mother to be quiet.

With home life so unsettled, I found a sense of peace in sports. I played mostly baseball and basketball. I was always the smallest kid on the team, but I made up for a lack of size with quickness and hustle. By age 12, I was certain I wanted to be a professional baseball player. I was a decent left-handed pitcher. My friend's father, who had played minor league ball, taught me a good move to first base. The first time I tried it I faked out our first baseman, and the ball went out into right field. I was known to walk many a batter, only to pick them off on the next play.

Pitching at Potomac Woods Park, Rockville, MD circa 1972

Potomac Woods Park, Rockville MD circa 1972

Unfortunately, everyone around me was growing, but I wasn't. When we moved up to the larger fields, I couldn't keep pitching at the further distance. I moved to the outfield and played up until 10th grade. I also found success in basketball. Twice, I was awarded MVP in my age group at Lefty Driesell's youth basketball camp. Playing sports allowed me to focus on the moment and, since I was good, it gave me a boost of self-esteem.

As a boy, if I wasn't playing sports, I was likely riding my bike – everywhere. There were no limits to where I could, or could not, go as long as I was home for dinner. A group of us would ride our bikes until we were lost, and then we tried to find our way home. We would ride on paths, through the woods, and come out at the other end on a road we weren't familiar with. One day, when I was about 13, our group rode our bikes about 15 miles to Washington DC, and took a tour at the FBI building. None of us told our parents where we were going.

At age 14, I planned to ride my bike 150 miles to Ocean City. Sound familiar? There were about eight kids who were interested in our adventurous trip but, by the time we were ready to go, only two of our parents were crazy enough to let us do it. I planned the route using side roads for most of the way. My dad, who must have understood my adventurous spirit, drove the path to confirm the roads were safe. He also tried to dissuade us from going through with it, though he was unsuccessful.

A few weeks later, my friend and I left Rockville on our bikes, and headed east with no parental supervision. The first leg was about 60 miles to the Chesapeake Bay Bridge, and it took us around five hours to get there, including breaks. Dad was away on business, so my older brother met us at the Bay Bridge and, since no bikes were allowed, drove us over it. He dropped us off on the other side, and drove ahead to set up a tent about 15 miles down the road at a state park. This was about 75 miles away from home, and a little over the halfway point of our journey. Unfortunately, the next day I got hurt. We were about eight miles from the beach, and I was riding with no hands. My front tire went over a rock, and I soared over the handlebars and landed on my shoulder. We didn't continue our grand biking adventure as a stranger, who witnessed the crash, drove us the rest of the way to Bethany Beach where my brother was waiting. He took me to a local doctor, and I was diagnosed with a separated shoulder. Needless to say, the return trip was by car.

Our family didn't know how to deal with my mother's illness, and we had limited emotional support from family and friends. My older sister lived in California, and tried to help by having Mom visit her and stay in a group home, but that didn't last long. My grandmother came to stay with us for several months, and she also left. It was too difficult for her to see her daughter in such a condition.

By the time I reached 10th grade, things at home were worse. My father had regular phone calls with my mom's brother, who was trying to set up a trust fund for her, bypassing my father. The conversations were loud, mainly my dad yelling at my uncle. My dad was also away from home on business trips more often, leaving me and my younger sister at home, with our mother, to fend for ourselves since my older siblings were grown and out of the house. We did have someone come over and cook meals from Monday through Thursday. But it was hard.

In February 1976, when I was 15 years old, I reached a point where I told Dad I couldn't take it anymore; I was moving to Las Vegas with a friend. His mother lived there. Dad wanted me to wait until the end of the school year. But a few days later, my friend and I ran away. We took a Greyhound bus from Rockville all the way to Las Vegas.

Surprisingly, our fathers allowed us to stay out there. But two weeks later, my friend got caught shoplifting, and we were sent back. We returned to Rockville by bus. I was welcomed home, and my dad let me have a phone in my room. My sister sent me a skateboard from California. I was starting to feel better about being home though, because the alternative in Las Vegas was not any better. My friend's mother was an alcoholic, and would come home intoxicated and yell at us.

When I returned home, I had to rearrange my classes, and many teachers didn't want me in their classrooms. I was considered too much trouble. However, one teacher in particular, Linda Crosslin, continued to believe in me and, because of her support, I made it through the next two years of high school. We later became lifelong friends.

But my sense of adventure I'd enjoyed in my youth had taken a back seat to the anxieties of adolescence. It would take a while before it would resurface again.

CHAPTER 3

▪ ▪ ▪ ▪

Finding Myself

> When I was a child, I talked like a child, I thought
> like a child, I reasoned like a child. When I became
> a man, I put childish ways behind me.
>
> 1 COR. 13:11

Growing up in a chaotic home, especially during adolescence, took a toll on my psyche. By the time I reached adulthood, I lacked confidence. My God-given gifts went untapped because they never received proper nurturing. Starting at age 13, I was pretty much on my own, so my self-esteem never developed. Still, growing up in a difficult environment did bring some rewards and hidden strengths. I had unknowingly developed an extraordinary amount of perseverance and determination. No one, except myself, could stop me from pursuing what I wanted.

As a teenager, I abandoned my dream of playing professional baseball, and decided I wanted to be a lawyer. Years later I would realize that my strong feelings against injustice had directed me to this career. In 9th grade, my science teacher was the victim of my relentless negotiating, as I maneuvered ways to get out of trouble. My dad would also challenge me:

"Aren't there too many lawyers?" he'd ask me.

"Yes," I would answer, following it up with, "But there's always room for a good lawyer."

Unfortunately, I didn't have the grades to attract any colleges. I had barely made it through high school, and I wasn't ready for the rigors of college. So, I took two gap years.

I landed a job with a police fundraising group that turned out to be just what I needed. It gave me an opportunity to get out of the house, as the group moved from town to town staying in hotels. It also helped me develop some confidence over the phone. I developed a good phone voice. I would speak louder and deeper than my normal voice and, eventually, it became more natural. Thanks to that job, I had the opportunity to travel to a lot of places – New York City; Beacon, New York; Norristown, Pennsylvania; Scranton/Wilkes-Barre, Pennsylvania; Rochester, New York; Lorain Ohio; Williamsport, Pennsylvania; and Canton Ohio. Getting out into the world felt like a breath of fresh air, away from the daily stress and tension at home. It freed up my mind to think more clearly, a freedom I had not felt before.

After being on the road for about 18 months, I was ready for college. I had reached a level of maturity physically, mentally, and emotionally. I believed I could take on the responsibility of getting a degree. And, although my parents expected all of us kids to go to college, I knew that a college degree and becoming a lawyer was my goal, not theirs.

Since I was a Maryland resident, and did fairly well on the SATs, I was accepted into the University of Maryland. (I wouldn't be as fortunate today.) Having never developed any study habits in high school, it took a couple years to learn how to study and write. It was trial-and-error as I watched those around me study. Once, I went to the writing center to learn basic paragraph structure. That helped me get decent grades in English. The determination and persistence I had acquired growing up, was put into practice. My grades picked up significantly during my junior and senior years, allowing me to continue my pursuit of becoming a lawyer. Although I didn't have a particular law school in mind, I knew I wanted to attend school somewhere I could stay and start my career. That was the general advice I had received from my career advisor. It also peaked my sense of adventure.

While I was in my sophomore year at the University of Maryland, my mother died. Dad called to tell me he found her at the kitchen table, with her head in the plate, and he got her out of the chair and put her on the floor. She had choked to death while eating[1]. Although I was extremely sad, I remember thinking that my mother was no longer suffering, and that brought a sense of relief. The suffering was also over for my dad, who stayed in the marriage, even though there hadn't been any intimacy or closeness for years.

My mom's death didn't derail me from my goals, and I was on track to graduate. It was a great day when I walked across the stage as a college graduate. After the University of Maryland, I took a year to work and mentally prepare for law school. I decided to participate in a triathlon. What better way to prepare for law school than to discipline myself to exercise six days a week, and push myself physically! I was working as a file clerk at a law firm in DC and rode my bike 15 miles to work, three days a week. When I started to train for the swimming part of the triathlon, I couldn't swim more than a few laps without stopping. Soon I learned how to breathe

---

[1] choking to death is a potential, though rare, complication for people with MS due to swallowing difficulties (dysphagia) and weakened muscles, leading to aspiration pneumonia.

correctly, and I steadily increased my distance. There was something about training, even when I didn't feel like it, that has helped me in all areas of my life, but especially when getting ready to attend law school. After completing the triathlon, I was ready for anything.

I headed west to attend California Western School of Law in San Diego. I had decided to take the advice of my career advisor, and attend school in an area where I thought I might want to live after graduating. What better place than San Diego, where it's sunny 300 days a year! It's one of the only big cities in the United States that is only a few minutes away from the ocean.

I drove a U-Haul truck 3,000 miles across the country by myself, stopping along the way to visit friends and family. Upon arrival, I quickly found a two-bedroom apartment near the school. It was perfect as I could ride my bike to school each day. I posted an ad for a roommate, and soon received a call from Mark Van Buskirk, a rancher from New Mexico, who was also attending the law school. He was starting a second career, so he was much older than me. As we talked, he happened to mention he was a born-again Christian. I was apprehensive about that.

My parents had always gone to church, and I attended up until my teenage years. I always believed in God, and my parents had told me we go to Heaven when we die, but I didn't have a sense of how faith affected my daily life. Most of the time, I reached out to God as a last resort. Otherwise, I believed I could take care of myself.

If I had taken the time to really think about it, I would have said I was angry with God for having a mother who was ill. But that perspective came years later. As I was entering law school, I hadn't processed any of that. I was just hoping that someone else might respond to the ad, someone besides Mark. But no one else did. So, the born-again Christian from New Mexico, became my roommate.

During that year, we had many conversations about Christianity, and God in general. The conversations were more like debates at times. But we were two law students discussing religion. I was troubled by the thought that becoming a Christian was the only way to Heaven. My parents never clarified what it meant to be a Christian. I had so many questions. What about those who never hear about Jesus? Or those who grow up in a different religion? As a logical thinker, it didn't make sense to me.

But, despite my questions and hesitations, living with Mark taught me a lot about faith. I watched how he lived out his faith each day. He always prayed silently before meals, even when he ate alone. On Sunday, he did not study at all, but he rested. With all the work required as a first-year law student, I didn't know how he did it. I never saw him get angry, and he never had a harsh word for anyone. He not only talked the talk, he walked the walk. After that first year, he transferred to a law school in New Mexico. But something had rubbed off on me. I began to attend church.

The next two years of law school went by quickly. Keeping busy tends to do that. As a full-time law student, there wasn't much free time – especially since I was committed to getting good grades. I also was becoming all too aware that, to be a practicing lawyer, I had to pass the two-day bar exam. Law school was more of a means to an end, although I knew there was a direct correlation between doing well in school and passing the bar. I was determined to pass the bar the first time around. The bar passage rate in California was around 60 percent, and Cal Western was committed to increasing its bar passage rate. I wanted to be one of its students to pass it the first time.

Although most of my time went to studying, I did go to church each week. The pastor was very personable, and I even took classes to join the church. But I still didn't know what it meant to be a Christian. The church I attended didn't press me on what I believed, and no one said I needed to do anything to become a Christian. I enjoyed going to church, and I was usually inspired by the sermon. But not much changed in my life.

During my third year of law school, at Christmas break, I made a big decision. I had considered living on the West coast after school, but I decided to return to the East coast after graduation. I really enjoyed San Diego but, after three years in paradise, I realized I was too far from home. My relationship with my dad was good, and I still had a lot of friends who stayed in the Washington DC area. Also, I really did like the change of seasons. Perhaps, if I had met the girl of my dreams out west, I may have stayed out there, but this God I was starting to learn more about had other plans for me in mind.

Graduation from Cal Western School of Law – 5/10/1988

CHAPTER 4

A New Creation

> Therefore if anyone is in Christ, he is a new
> creation; the old has gone, the new has come!
>
> 2 COR. 5:17

I did it! In May 1988, I returned home to Maryland with my father who had flown to San Diego for my graduation. We drove back in a car that I had purchased after my first year in law school. We stopped along the way in Colorado Springs and, of course, in Chicago to see a Cubs' game. Even though my dad would have wanted to see more sights, I needed to get back home so I could study for the bar exam. For the next six weeks, I studied for approximately eight hours per day, seven days a week and, toward the last few weeks, it was more like twelve hours per day. A little overkill but, in the end, I became a part of the 70 percent (a bit higher rate than California), and I passed the Maryland bar the first time around! I was officially a lawyer! But that wasn't the only new identity I was experiencing.

After my mother died, my dad got more active in his faith. He attended National Presbyterian Church in Washington DC, where the well-known Louis Evans pastored. I had gone with him a few times when I was home for the holidays. When I moved back, Dad told me Fourth Presbyterian Church in Bethesda, Maryland, had a large singles' group called Ambassadors. I began to attend it in the spring of 1989. Every Sunday there were at least 300 single people in attendance, and well over half were women. This was the first time I was around so many young people committed to their faith. The focus was clearly on God, and I was beginning to see how differently both the men and women lived their lives. They acted a lot like my law school roommate, Mark. One day after Sunday school, I asked the guest speaker a question. Although I don't remember exactly how I phrased it, he must have known I didn't understand what it meant to be a Christian, because he asked to meet for lunch later that week.

His name was Spencer Brand. We met at a nice restaurant, and I wasn't sure the purpose of the meeting, but I figured that since he was a speaker at our church, it was worth my time for us to get together. At lunch, he quickly explained the gospel; that we are all sinners, and God sent his only son Jesus Christ as a sacrifice so we may be reconciled to God. As a result, all our sins are forgiven. But first I needed to confess my sins, and ask Jesus into my heart. Finally, I understood. Faith isn't a one-time event, but the beginning of a relationship with Christ, a new life in Christ. It became clear that it wasn't for me to decide who goes to Heaven. That is up to God. But I also realized God had been working on me, ever since he put Mark and I as roommates three years prior. God used Spencer, and our lunch, to bring me to Christ. I accepted Christ into my heart that day, May 11, 1989.

As a new believer, I began to read my Bible and pray. I also developed friendships with both men and women in Ambassadors, going on fall and spring retreats and joining a men's Bible study. I continued to grow in my faith and learn more about what it meant to be a Christian. I quickly realized there were some things in my life I needed to change.

Although I wasn't a heavy drinker, I had occasionally drunk too much, so I vowed to no longer get drunk because the Bible (Ephesians 5:18) says, 'Do not get drunk on wine which leads to debauchery. Instead, be filled with the Spirit.' I took that seriously.

I also had no opinion about sex before marriage but, after becoming a Christian, I vowed to not have sex until I was married. I felt I was really listening to God for the first time in my life.

During this time, I also began questioning whether God wanted me to be a lawyer. I thought perhaps God had something else in mind for me, and I wanted to be open to it. But I soon realized God knew I was going to be a lawyer, and He knew I wasn't going to be a Christian until after I finished law school. And God knows, we could always use more honest, caring lawyers! So I continued to pursue my law career.

For two years, I attended Ambassadors, and grew in my faith. With over 300 people attending every Sunday, it took a while to meet everyone. But, in May 1991, I was at a church retreat at a 4-H center where there was a large kitchen, dining area, separate sleeping quarters for men and women, and a large conference room for worship music and the speaker. All who attended were assigned to a small co-ed group, that met after the large session, to discuss the topic and pray. A woman named Marie was one of the group leaders, and I noticed her as she carried a sign with the name of her group on it so people could find her. I wasn't in her group, but I found myself sitting next to her and we had a brief conversation. She was very beautiful and clearly had a heart for God. I was a bit intimidated because she was a group leader. However, I had just started dating someone else, who wasn't in the Ambassadors' group, so I didn't pay her as much attention as I would have otherwise. Marie did invite me to go hiking with a group of people, but I declined and said I was planning to play soccer.

Our paths didn't cross again until August, when I happened to notice her across the room on a Sunday morning at Ambassadors. She looked even more beautiful. I thought she looked back at me. Since I was no longer in a relationship, I located her phone number in the Ambassadors' directory, and gave her a call. I got her answering machine, and left her a message. She called me back the next night, but I missed her call.

I had begun keeping a journal as my faith grew. As a Christian, it was a way to track my spiritual growth. I would write any insights about what God was teaching me. The journal was also a way to record my general thoughts and feelings. It helped me identify areas of strengths and weaknesses, destructive patterns that prevented me from closer relationships, and my motives.

8/14/1991

Marie called back at 9:30 pm and left me a message. I'm not sure why I didn't hear the phone. She said she was going to bed early – so I didn't call her back. She sounded as if she knew who I was – I remember we had eye contact three weeks ago, she seemed to give me a look. I was strong, and didn't call her back. Will call her tomorrow and ask her out for next week – remember at the retreat she asked me to go hiking.

I called her the next night.

>Dave: "Do you want to do something?"
>Marie: "What did you have in mind?"

Dave: "I don't know. I'll get back to you next week."

I journaled later that I should have been more direct. I didn't take charge. When I called her back, we decided to meet up after church and go to a park in Virginia for a civil war reenactment. It turned out that two of Marie's friends were already planning to go to this event, and we all went together.

Even though she agreed to go, she later admitted she wasn't really sure who I was. She said it was my phone voice that persuaded her!

We started officially dating at the end of August 1991. From the start of our relationship, she was different from other women. For one, she always returned my calls! She was very responsive, without appearing too interested. We were both attracted to each other's commitment to faith, and our times together were natural as we got to know one another.

Although we lived an hour apart, we managed to see each other three to four times per week, meeting for dinner, attending church events, going dancing, and attending the fall retreat. She had been in two long relationships but, in each case, they had ended because she desired to find a man of strong faith. Although Marie tends to be indecisive at times, she was ready to get married, and recognized my heart for God. We both believed God had brought us together. He had done a lot of work in me to get me to a place where Marie would be attracted to me. Once my heart was surrendered to Him, God brought Marie into my life. By November of 1991, we were engaged.

My faith was growing, and I'd met my future wife. A lot was happening! Yet my sense of adventure and risk was alive and well, as I decided to start my own law practice at the beginning of 1992. I had been working for a prominent criminal defense attorney for two years, but he wasn't willing to increase my salary, and I was beginning to build my own client base. Most importantly, I wanted to decide how to represent my clients, and practice law as a Christian attorney, which would include praying with and for my clients.

Opening my own firm would be the first sign to my soon-to-be wife that I was willing to take risks, and not worry about failing. It didn't scare her away. We planned our wedding, and were married on May 23, 1992.

May 23, 1992 – Beverley Hills Church, Alexandria, Va
My dad is in the background – he was my best man

CHAPTER 5

Starting a Family and a Law Practice

> For I know the plans I have for you, declares
> the Lord, plans to prosper you and not to harm
> you, plans to give you hope and a future.
>
> JER. 29:11

O ur first few years of marriage were more than your typical learning experience. Since we dated for such a short time, we only saw each other's strengths, but somehow managed to miss each other's weaknesses. The first glimpse of our differences started on the second day of marriage when we were at the airport, ready to go to St. Kitts in the Caribbean for our honeymoon. I had brought my birth certificate, but it was only a copy, and the airline said I needed a certified copy. The ticket agent eventually said we could take the chance and leave, but she wasn't sure if we would be allowed to return to the country. I was ready to take the chance, but not Marie. Finally, the employee at the counter called the St. Kitts airport, and they agreed to accept a copy. It was our first lesson in learning how very different we are when it comes to taking risks.

Honeymoon – St. Kitts

Making decisions together was also difficult for us at first. We found out years later that I am a get-it-done person, and Marie is a get-it-right person. It was challenging. But, thanks to a personality test, we learned the ways we each needed to stretch and get out of our comfort zones to make the relationship work. More importantly, we shared similar values, and a commitment to living out our faith in our marriage. Early on, we began to compromise.

Prior to getting married, we each owned condos, and we had each agreed to sell them, and move closer to a midpoint between our jobs. Originally from Virginia, Marie was living there when we got married, and she was also working on her master's in social work. Since I sold my condo first, I moved in with her in Virginia, which created an hour-long commute each way to work in Rockville. We then sold her condo, and rented a home in Falls Church, Virginia, so she could finish school and I could shorten my commute. I drove back and forth to Rockville (about a 30-minute drive without traffic, and an hour-and-a-half drive with traffic), where I had begun my law practice as a solo practitioner.

We also knew we weren't getting any younger. I was 32 and Marie was 29, and we knew we wanted kids. We decided to start a family right away. Our first son, Jonathan, was born July 28, 1993, a little over a year after our wedding. I felt overwhelmed, and filled with joy at the same time. As parents, we were both committed to raising godly children. However, we had no idea how much time parenting would take. In fact, we spent the first three months of Jonathan's life trying to figure out how to get him to sleep!

Although the timing hadn't been great for me to venture out on my own, Marie was supportive, and we were working well together as first-time parents. Marie was still working on finishing her masters, which meant I needed to come home early a couple times a week to watch Jonathan. We continued to attend the same church, but we had graduated from Ambassadors and moved into a Young Married class. We were also in a Bible study with five other couples, and enjoyed building relationships with other young families. We had found a home to rent across the street from one of the couples in our Bible study.

After completing her master's in social work, Marie was ready to take a break from working, and her desire was to be a stay-at-home mom while the children were little. She was pregnant with our second child, and raising our one-year-old. So, my job was our only source of income. Unfortunately, it was taking longer than expected for me to build a client base, and Marie was getting a little nervous about the lack of steady salary. We struggled financially for two years before we had our first serious discussion about where my practice was headed. I told her if I didn't reach certain goals by the end of the year, I would look for a salaried position in a law firm.

> **4/30/95**
>
> Sat next to Frank Young (physician/teacher) at church; asked him about praying for direction – he said you must pray and start paddling, God will steer; also focus on where you can have the greatest impact using your gifts – don't focus on money, don't focus on amount of time away from home; as far as ability – ask colleagues; but don't think small.
>
> Begin making a list of thoughts that come to mind about career, and ask God to make it clear-and write down areas where you can make an impact in your community.

Those words from Frank Young[2] continued to resonate with me, and would later become very relevant. But at the moment, I was balancing my career goals with my family responsibilities. We had outgrown our rental house and, with another child on the way, it was time to move. At the same time, my father was struggling with living alone. His health was declining, and he was still living in the house I grew up in. We found a home that could accommodate all of us and, in April 1995, we bought a four-bedroom house. The home had three levels, with a finished basement that included a kitchen area, full bath and bedroom, where Dad would live. He joined us in June, just three months before our son Michael was born on

---

[2]   In 1995, Dr Young was serving as director of both the Office of Emergency Preparedness and the National Disaster Medical System during the Clinton Administration. Prior to that, he was commissioner of the FDA.

September 1, 1995. It was an exciting time in the Pasti household, despite being very overwhelmed.

8/31/95

Last three weeks have been nonstop – jury trial – very satisfied with performance, and learned a lot – preparation is everything – Marie has been on bedrest for two weeks – but we made it through, now we could have the baby any day. Anxiety about new baby – not mentally prepared yet; and concerned about healthy baby – no focus on God, except for praying with Marie.

I was trying to balance building my practice, helping Marie with the kids, and supporting my dad. He was mostly independent, but was dependent on us for most of his social activity. Marie and I were resigned to the fact our alone time was very limited. Thankfully, Marie's parents were only about 45 minutes away, so we could drop off the kids and have a night away once in a while.

Despite our hectic lives, I continued to pray about my career, and dream.

10/9/95

Continue to pray for direction from God in career, and continue to go forward. God speaks to those who speak to Him – through prayer; not because we are chosen or because we are special – but because we believe, and we come to God for answers with an expectation and willingness to wait for an answer.

My father was enjoying his time with us, and we believed we were doing the right thing by having him move in. I also enjoyed a much shorter commute to work (15 minutes each way), and Marie was home with the kids. I was home most every night for dinner, and Marie was trying to meet the needs of our kids and my father. But we were exhausted most of the time.

In November, the doctor put a shunt in Dad's arm, so he could begin dialysis at the beginning of 1996, but his health declined and, just over a month later, we were at his funeral and saying goodbye to a man who had been a source of strength for my life.

Losing my father was painful and traumatic. My mind was clouded in grief. But fortunately, by the end of that year, my third year in practice, I had met the goals Marie and I agreed upon. I could continue on my own.

It meant a lot to me to have my own practice. I could practice the way I wanted as Christian attorney. I applied biblical principles, like the Golden Rule; 'Do unto others as you would have them do unto you.' Most people are familiar with this rule, but some people don't know it was Jesus who said it. I also felt a responsibility to put each client's interests above my own. That was the oath I took as a lawyer, and I believed it. I was an attorney with ethics!

12/27/1995

Last two days have been well spent with retreat – a lot of discussions about plans/goals for the year – goals seem to be set, based on what was missing – so most of accomplishments will only make us more functional – such as organization – but will give us an opportunity to move in a forward direction – but nothing really creative or expansive goals – and not necessarily what God would have us do – but we will re-evaluate in three months. The mind of man plans his way, but the Lord directs his steps. Prov. 16:9

But there was another reason I liked working on my own. I remembered my father always complaining about his bosses at IBM, and I had subconsciously decided it would not be good to work for someone else. As I processed losing my dad, and looking ahead, I felt lost yet motivated to keep going.

Although losing Dad brought an unexpected turn of events, it led me to an answer to many of my questions and prayers.

CHAPTER 6

Searching for Significance

*Delight yourself in the Lord and he will
give you the desires of your heart.*

PSALM 37:4

Looking back on the night my father died, I am thankful we spent the last couple hours of his life together. Although it was extremely painful to watch him die, it was also a gift from God. I got to hear my dad's final thoughts about his life. As I slowly began to process my feelings, it wasn't only him passing away in my arms that affected me, but it was how he looked back on his life, with regret, during our last dinner together.

I have heard it said many times that most people, from their death bed, don't say they wish they would have spent more time at the office. Most of the time, and mostly men, regret they didn't spend more time with their kids. With my father, it was different. He poured his life into his four kids.

He would do anything for us. He was the one who drove my older sister to college at Wesleyan University in Connecticut, and my older brother to Northwestern University in Illinois. He even let me come along for the ride. When I drove back from San Diego after law school, my dad came with me. He believed in us. He came to most of my little league games, and I don't remember him ever saying anything negative about how I performed. He was the father with a Life Saver after the game, when things didn't go well. When he died, I lost my greatest cheerleader.

It was different when my mother died. The MS had affected her mind, and there was so much tension and suffering. When I received the call about mom's death, I was sad, but I mostly felt relieved that she was at peace and in a better place. But the death of a second parent is more devastating than I realized. And I was much closer to Dad.

Over the next several months after he died, I felt lost. I was not only grieving the death of my father, but also the harsh reality that I no longer had any living parents. The profound sense of loss went deeper, as I grieved never having a healthy family. As a teenager, I was on my own most of the time. That helped me to become more independent, but it didn't help me deal with my feelings. Now in my thirties, I was facing the same pain, but without coping skills.

I had a supportive wife who cared for me. She tried to get me to open up but, for a while, I couldn't express how I was feeling. I also learned we grieved differently from one another. I found peace just by cutting the grass and exercising. She gravitated toward talking about our feelings, and accepting support from others.

Not long after Dad died, Marie and I went through a grieving seminar presented at my father's church by a Christian counselor. It was in the Sunday school class my father attended, and most of the attendees knew him. The seminar helped me begin to process the loss. Marie and I also got together weekly with my brother and sister, and a brother-in-law who had recently lost one of his parents as well. As I let support come around me, I started to feel closer to others, and to God as well. Ultimately, I was learning that we have a Father in Heaven who cares for us, and we can take all our burdens to Him.

At some point during the grieving process, I reached a point when I could begin to focus on my career again. Since becoming a Christian, I had begun to be open to God's will for my life and I believed the verse in Jeremiah 29:11 – 'I know the plans for you says the Lord.' I had remembered what Frank Young told me about paddling and praying for God to steer, and I was ready to channel my energy toward finding purpose. I also began to look at what I was most passionate about. I flipped back through my journal entries, and one from September 1996, jumped out. It was related to becoming a sports' agent.

9/12/96

Thoughts about representing athletes, using negotiating skills, and doing something that I would like.

Over the next six months, I considered other possibilities; like going into politics and becoming more involved in Peacemaker ministries, an organization founded by Ken Sande that focused on healthy ways to resolve conflict. But I kept coming back to becoming a sports' agent. As a kid, playing sports was always a place of peace for me. That was where I could get lost in the moment, and just focus on the game. It's how I made new friends when we moved. It's how I found the confidence I needed, when self-esteem didn't come from home.

I knew what it took to be an athlete, so I felt that, as a sports' agent, I could relate to my clients. Just being around sports was an exciting thought. But could I trust my instincts? Was God putting this desire in me? Or was I following my own selfish desires? Whatever the reason, it was clear I had an untapped passion that was beginning to surface. My journal entries began filling up with these thoughts and dreams, questions about second-guessing myself, and my motives.

1/19/97

Began to have second thoughts about pursuing sports law- thinking; it's just a pipe dream – all because sports agent didn't call me back and $1,000 annual licensing fee to state. But I must continue to network, and to read and learn. I need to figure out who my clients will be, and what their needs are – need to educate myself on NCAA rules and Collective Bargaining Agreements; Contract Clauses; etc – but if this is my 10-year goal, I must be sure if I'm going to invest time and money (I was also thinking about politics – but I feel like I'm only drawn to the power and attention it would bring)

1/21/97

I do pray for confirmation that I should continue with sports law. In the meantime, continue to network. Am I doing sports law as a response to midlife crisis – and, if so, is that the wrong reason? But it has given me new energy and hope.

2/8/97

Did a career exercise and noticed that many of the qualities I want to express could be through politics, but on the other hand if I'm successful with sports law, I could have my own organization that empowers youth, and I could express myself through the organization.

2/11/97

For sports law, I do not have long term goals right now. Need to find out what I need to know. I do realize I need more than one person's perspective. Everyone's opinions are based on their own experiences.

2/18/97

Today I prayed about sports law, and a Sports Lawyers Assoc packet came with a directory – called law student in Rockville who is in St Louis now. His mother called and we talked for 30 minutes. It gave me new energy. I left a message with Prof Stiglitz, who is also a member of SLA.

3/8/97

I do need to step back and look at the big picture. Where do I want to be in 10 years?

4/30/97

Praying for career direction, especially after attending Peacemakers' seminar. I should at least follow through with conciliator program, as I am more interested in negotiation than litigation. Continue to take steps toward peacemaking, and see where God leads. And continue to pursue sports law, and see where God leads.

6/2/97

Kept a hectic pace for most days on vacation, but we all ran out of gas towards the end of the week; remember, the reason I went in the first place – to attend the sports lawyers conference. It was well worth it. I met several people who were willing to talk with me. It was hard to switch gears in the middle of vacation, but it was worth the sacrifice. However, I'm not refreshed for returning to work, especially since I'm motivated to go into sports law.

6/6/97

I am beginning to take hold of the baby step concept – having the big goal and breaking it down to monthly, weekly, daily goals. With sports law I am at the fact gathering stage, try not to get ahead of myself. For now, continue to talk with people and learn. Then set more specific goals – ones that can be accomplished – and build confidence that way.

> *7/9/97*
>
> *Certainly I can continue to pursue sports law, provided it doesn't take me away from God.*

> *7/14/97*
>
> *If we are not experiencing the much more of our Heavenly Father, it is because we are not obeying the life God has given us, we are taken up with confusing considerations (Chambers, My Utmost for His Highest 1/26).*

After months of grappling with questions and taking next steps, the key insight came on August 28, 1997.

> *8/28/97*
>
> *In discerning God's will with career, I keep coming back to glorifying God in whatever I do. It doesn't matter what I do, but how I do it. It's okay if I pursue sports law, but will it take me away from my family more? Will that be glorifying God less?*

Finally, after about a year of prayer, research, and seeking advice of others, I decided I wanted to explore becoming a sports' agent. I had always loved sports and, as a lawyer, I had become a skilled negotiator. Psalm 37:4 came to mind, 'Delight yourself in the Lord and He will give you the desires of your heart.' I felt God put this passion in my heart. I knew I had the skills to be an agent, and I believed I had the right motives. I decided I was ready to begin. The question was – how to start?

CHAPTER 7

Taking the Plunge

> I can accept failure, everyone fails at something.
> But I cannot accept not trying.
>
> MICHAEL JORDAN

My law practice had really taken off. I had advertised on a local Christian radio station, and the cases were coming in. I had begun taking steps toward becoming a sports' agent, but I had very little discretionary time. Then one day I received a letter from a third-year law student, Charles "Chip" Lipscomb. I had met him at the Sports Lawyers Conference, and he was looking for a job. I was impressed with his energy. He was one of the seminar speakers, and gave a talk titled, 'How to break into the sports industry.' However, he hadn't really done much, as he was still in law school. Still, he convinced me he could help.

Chip started working for me in August 1998. I paid him a salary so, from the start, he was an expense. I figured he could free up some of my time by handling some law cases, and he could also spend time developing our sports' practice. It didn't take long for Chip to go in all sorts of directions. He was in contact with a female sailor, an Olympic rower, and a field goal kicker with a semi-pro team. I gave him some leeway, but those clients weren't going to produce revenue anytime soon.

I started in another direction, as I received a call from an undrafted basketball player, Curtiss Johnson, who had heard my ad on the Christian radio station. He had played for the hall of famer Rick Barry, in an Independent league. I left a message with the team, and Rick actually returned my call. I tried to act like it wasn't a big deal, but it was a big deal! I was trying to find out from Rick if Curtiss was worth pursuing, and he had a lot of good things to say. Subsequently, Curtiss told me there were openings for a team in Winnipeg. I was able to arrange a tryout with Darryl Dawkins, the former NBA player who was coaching the Winnipeg team. I drove with Curtiss and his wife to New Jersey, so Darryl could get a look at Curtiss.

We went to a high school gym near Darryl's home. They needed an extra player, so I was the point guard feeding the ball to my player, who was being covered by Darryl. That was a familiar position for me, having played point guard throughout my early years. Curtiss performed well enough to get invited to the team's official tryouts, but unfortunately he injured his hamstring and didn't make the team. But it gave me a taste of the possibilities.

Although I didn't realize it at the time, hiring Chip had created some urgency for income to cover the additional expense. We were moving forward at an incredible pace. Well, at least we were moving, but I don't know about the forward part. The problem was we weren't directing our attention to any particular sport, and we were going in too many directions.

Our focus turned to baseball as we felt we had a better chance of getting some minor league players. It's different in basketball and football, where the player is drafted and immediately goes to the NBA and NFL. In baseball, with a few rare exceptions, the player starts in the minors, at the lowest level, and works their way up from rookie ball to Low A, High A, AA, AAA and then to the Majors. The normal progression is a level each year for a high school player. For a college player, they may skip a level. On average, a player who is destined for the Majors will spend four to six years in the minors.

We started to reach out to college and high school coaches, to get a feel for the local talent. Also, Chip knew a baseball agent who was getting out of the business. He referred us to our first two baseball clients, Allen Shrum and Tim Cossins.

Unfortunately, what we didn't know at the time was that most minor league players were not considered prospects. Each year there are 50 rounds in the annual baseball draft[3], and usually, with some exceptions, most players become filler players after the 10th round. Each team must find other players to fill different positions so the prospects can play. They are also known as organizational players. There are only a few Major League prospects on most lower-level minor league teams. Unfortunately, both Allen and Tim fell into the non-prospect category.

Still, as we were continuing to learn the business, it was important to find some clients. Even a non-prospect could lead us to other players. We concluded it was better to have a non-prospect than to have no players. You never know where it might lead.

It didn't take long before we had our third client, Tim Hamulack. He had just finished his third season in pro ball. Up to that point, he had made it to Low A ball. Two years at rookie level, and then one season at Low A. Certainly not on the quick path to the Majors. Still, he was a left-handed pitcher, who threw 90 MPH, and that wasn't easy to find in 1998.

---

[3] In 2021, the draft was reduced to 20 rounds. Also, in 2020, MLB restructured the minor leagues, cutting ties with 40 affiliated teams.

Meeting Tim was a serendipity moment that all dream chasers need. Perhaps it was God's way of saying I was on the right path. Marie and I just happened to be on the same cruise ship as Tim's girlfriend's parents. It was a cruise on the Potomac River in Washington DC for those who advertised on the local Christian radio station. The couple was in the termite business, so a conversation with them would have only lasted a few minutes at most. But, when asked what I did, I mentioned I was starting to represent baseball players. They said their daughter's boyfriend was looking for an agent. What are the chances?! I learned an important lesson – no matter who I'm talking to, let them know I'm a baseball agent.

We soon picked up two more players, whom Tim Cossins had referred. Brad Elwood, a catcher, was a 20th round pick out of West Virginia, and Brandon Agamennone, a pitcher, was also a 20th round pick out of the University of Maryland. Both players resided in Maryland. We figured it was beneficial to represent players from local colleges because they could lead us to other players who had good character and were considered prospects.

We were pursuing a successful sports' agency, and we wanted clients striving to be amazing athletes, all of us setting big goals and pursuing God-sized dreams.

CHAPTER 8

The Annual Baseball Draft

> All of our dreams can come true if we
> have the courage to pursue them.
>
> WALT DISNEY

The baseball draft is held each year in the first or second week of June. It is the beginning of the dream for those whose goal it is to be a Major League baseball player. With some exceptions, high school seniors, and those who have completed their junior year of college, are eligible to be drafted. Unlike other sports, the player does not need to declare his eligibility.

Chip and I soon discovered that we could earn some money by representing players in the draft. In 1999, the top player drafted, Josh Hamilton, signed for $3.9 million dollars. That's just for signing. A commission of 3 to 4% for almost any player, drafted in the first round, would cover my entire salary for the year. Unfortunately, with the intense competition among agents to secure the top talent, it was next to impossible for a small agency like ours, with no known players, to get a first-round player. Every year the same agencies had players in the first few rounds of the draft. Still, the signing bonus for players drafted in rounds 3 to 5 was in the $200,000 to $400,000 range. We figured we had a realistic chance of getting those players. More importantly, unlike many minor league players, these players did not yet have agents.

First, we had to find out how to identify the prospects, and then to represent them in the draft. A starting source was *Baseball America*, a magazine devoted entirely to baseball. It was recommended to me by an attorney at the Sports Lawyers Conference, and it proved to be a good resource. Each year, *Baseball America* lists the nation's top 100 high school seniors, and top 100 college draft eligible players.

We began to focus on players in the Mid-Atlantic region, which included Maryland, Delaware, Pennsylvania, West Virginia, Virginia, and Washington DC. It was easier for us to focus on players within a 200-mile radius. That enabled us to see them play, and have a better chance at developing relationships with them. Although our region was not a hot bed for baseball, there were enough prospects to keep us busy. There was also less competition compared to Florida, Texas, and California, where the majority of prospects were located and, not surprisingly, they could play baseball all year long. (Maybe not so good for pitchers.)

Most of the top high school players in the region played on travel teams in the fall. As we began to attend these games, we noticed Major League scouts at some of them. That's always a good sign. We began to introduce ourselves to the scouts, and slowly developed relationships. Some would be forthcoming with information, while others wouldn't talk much. There was a part-time scout who befriended us, and helped identify the top talent in the area. From there we would send a letter to the family, explaining the draft process and how we could help as their advisor.

The NCAA has a clause that says an athlete can seek advice from counsel regarding a professional contract. Thus, the term 'advisor' came into existence. The NCAA also makes it clear that an athlete cannot have an agent. An agent is defined as someone who markets the player's talents to Major League teams. We would spend a lot of time educating families about the differences between an advisor and an agent. In most instances, it was in title only, but it was hard for families to understand they could have someone represent their sons. Most families soon learned that, when they didn't have anyone to advise them, they were at an extreme disadvantage.

We set our sights on the 1999 draft, and found a few players to contact. My first big meeting was with a potential 3rd round pick, Joe Saunders. I had previously met his coach at West Springfield High School, Coach Tugwell, who helped arrange a meeting with Joe's family. The Saunders were good people but, unfortunately, after the meeting I realized I didn't know much about the draft, and how I could help with the draft process. Joe would end up going with another agency and, although he was drafted in the 5th round, he didn't sign and went to Virginia Tech instead. Three years later, he was drafted in the 1st round, and eventually became an established pitcher in the Majors.

After the meeting with Joe, I contacted an agent who I had met at the annual Sports Lawyers Conference. We had graduated from the same law school, and he had a pretty good handle on the draft. I paid him $2,500 as a consultant, and to teach me about the draft. I was impressed because he had advised a player in the 1st round of the previous draft.

He taught me about the draft process, and the role of an advisor. The need for an advisor arose because of the nature of the baseball draft. If a team is interested in drafting a player, they will contact the player well before the draft and ask them a lot of questions. The team is trying to determine if the player will sign if drafted. Each round had what was called 'round money,' and each round had a signing bonus range. If a team saw the player as a 3rd round pick, and the player wanted 1st round money, that player would be considered an unsignable player and, more likely than not, he would not be drafted. Or, in some cases, a team would take a flyer on him (draft him in the later rounds) and see if his demands would come down.

An advisor steps in to help a player with their market value, and how to respond to the teams' questions. If a player is interested in signing, an advisor tells them that if they want to be drafted, they may need to lower their expectations. Unfortunately, many families do not understand the process. They may say they're going to wait until after the draft to see if they need help.

However, most of what happens in the draft is a function of what happens before the draft. It's the job of each team to determine the player's signability, and the area scout is responsible for finding out, from the player, what it would take to sign. If they don't know, or won't respond, they probably won't be drafted unless the scout has a good sense that the player will sign if drafted. But they usually won't be drafted in the top rounds, for fear of wasting a pick.

Another factor we considered for the high school prospects was the value of college scholarships. If a player is signed for a full scholarship to Stanford, Vanderbilt, or Virginia, it's going to take more money than a player who has a scholarship to a less expensive or less academic school, irrespective of the player's value. As is the case with the value of our houses, most of the time, player's families believe their sons have higher values than the market dictates.

With this newfound knowledge in hand, I set up a meeting with a potential 1st round pick, Jimmy Gobble. His family lived in Bristol, Virginia, about six hours from my home. His father had contacted me in response to a letter I sent, where I mentioned it would be better to have a lawyer represent them, as opposed to just an agent.

The family lived in a mobile home in the country. This meeting was better than my first meeting with Joe, but I didn't make a connection with the player. I had learned that the connection, and trust, between athlete and advisor was just as important as my ability to represent him, so I knew when I left that they weren't going to hire me. Jimmy ended up being drafted in the supplemental 1st round, and signed for $720,000. I was happy for him and his family.

After all was said and done, we ended up with two college seniors in the 1999 draft – Tom Curtiss at the University of Maryland, and Chris Warren from Howard University. Both signed for $1,000. These were known as "Senior signs." They weren't drafted as juniors, because teams weren't willing to pay enough to buy them out of their last year of college. Through this process, Chip and I learned another lesson – Senior signs are not usually prospects.

As we learned the ropes of drafting players and advising them, we learned the key to being drafted is making yourself a signable player. A player's value cannot exceed the team's value for them. It was our job to determine the player's market value. And, the best way to determine market value, is by attending the games. If a team is interested in a player, an area scout will be at some, or most, of their games. The higher the player's value, the more we would see cross-checkers (a scout who compares players from different regions) and even the scouting director for those considered in the top rounds.

This is what appealed to me as a sports' agent. Ever since I was a kid, I loved attending baseball games. Games became a good way to meet a player's family, and show them we were interested in helping their son. The baseball field became our office. Also, it was a reminder of all the baseball games I went to with my dad, especially at Wrigley Field in Chicago when we would visit my grandmother there.

But going to games meant being away from home, and that was not what Marie had expected when I originally mentioned this career change. At the time, she was expecting child number three. We had many conversations about compromise and expectations as my sports' agency grew.

CHAPTER 9

Finally: A Prospect

Formula for success: Rise early, work hard, strike oil.

J. PAUL GETTY

With the 1999 draft in the books, we quickly set our sights on the 2000 draft. With a better understanding of how things worked, and some additional contacts, we had a much better chance of finding the prospects sooner. We identified several top prospects in our area. The top players included Randy Truselo, a high school player from Delaware; Chris Russ, a college player at Towson, Maryland; Kenny Nelson, a high school player at Riverdale Baptist in Maryland; Taylor Buchholz, a high school player from Springfield, Pennsylvania; and Gerald Oakes, a high school player from Media, Pennsylvania.

During the spring and summer of 1999, Chip and I watched these players, and developed relationships with their families. During spring training in Florida, I saw Kenny Nelson pitch, as Riverdale Baptist played in a tournament during spring break. I had developed a relationship with Riverdale

FINALLY: A PROSPECT

Baptist's coach, and he made me feel welcome when I attended the game. Chip watched Taylor Buchholz a few times, and introduced himself to his parents. By the end of the summer, we had inroads with all the players on our list, and we began to set up meetings with the families.

As a practicing lawyer for ten years, I didn't see myself as a salesman. When I meet a first-time client for my law practice, I explain the process and they quickly get the sense I know what I'm doing. When I went to give a presentation to a baseball family on how I could help, I used the same approach, but it wasn't as easily received. There was much more selling involved, especially since the families usually met with several advisors before deciding who to work with.

We gave it our best shot with Randy Truselo's family, but he was ranked by *Baseball America* as the 10th best high school prospect in the country. By the time we made it to his living room, they must have met with at least ten other agents. Still, we gave a great presentation, with charts and predictions, of who might take him. They were impressed, but not impressed enough. Oddly enough, they went with someone who had no players in the Majors, and no players drafted in the top rounds in the draft.

We were fortunate with Taylor Buchholz's family. Taylor was not as highly regarded as the others on our list, so he wasn't getting the same kind of attention from other agents. Still, Taylor was ranked #91 in *Baseball America's* top high school prospects, so he wasn't an unknown either. According to *Baseball America*, he was projected in the 3rd to 5th round range. Chip and I met with the Buchholz family in the fall of 1999, just after the birth of my third child, Sammy, born November 10, 1999.

Not only was I on a high from becoming a father again, but I had a good feeling. It was Thanksgiving weekend. The Buchholz's liked the fact Chip and I were lawyers, and it appeared they were looking for someone they could trust. We left the meeting encouraged, but knowing we would need to wait until the spring to know our fate, and if any prospects chose to hire us.

In the meantime, we continued to follow up by sending letters and staying in touch. We also attended a few winter showcase events to show our continued support and interest. Finally, in the early March of 2000, we got the news. We had lost out on Kenny Nelson, Randy Truselo, and Chris Russ. But we were in with Taylor Buchholz! Gerald Oakes' family had decided to wait but, since he lived near Taylor, we would continue to follow him as well. We were elated.

It was approximately two hours and twenty minutes from my office to Springfield, Pennsylvania. I made that trip four times to see Taylor pitch. Taylor had a good fastball, consistently in the low 90s, and he showed a decent curveball. He had good command of his pitches, and he dominated his competition. At 6ft 3, he was a good size, but the scouts said he had a bad body, mainly because he carried a little extra baby fat around his midsection. This was attributed to his need for extra weight when he played as his school's quarterback.

Taylor had a scholarship to North Carolina, so he had some leverage. He would soon have to decide what it would take for him to forgo college. That's where I came in. Taylor's father knew that, having an advisor, sent a message to the teams that he was interested in signing a professional contract. But he also knew a scholarship to North Carolina was a pretty good alternative. As their advisor, I made it clear that the decision of whether or not to sign was up to Taylor. I was simply going to give them good information to help them decide. I wasn't going to push Taylor to sign, as some advisors do.

Based on my assessment of Taylor's value, I believed Taylor wouldn't be drafted higher than the 3rd round. Although several crosscheckers came in to see Taylor, he didn't get the attention of any scouting directors. Based

FINALLY: A PROSPECT

on his body, and an average Major League fastball, I was confident in my prediction. Mr. Buchholz agreed, and began to tell scouts it would take $400,000 to sign Taylor. If he had wanted more than that, I believe teams would have said, "We'll see you in three years." Yet even with that amount, there were many teams who considered him unsignable. The pie was getting smaller.

Just prior to the draft, Taylor was invited to a pre-draft workout with the Phillies, his hometown team. Taylor caught the eye of Mike Arbuckle, the scouting director, who clocked Taylor at 94 MPH on a few pitches. A few days later he called Taylor during the draft, and asked if he would take $375,000 to sign. He replied in the affirmative, and was taken in the 6th round.

I would not know until several years later but, out of all the prospects we met with that year, Taylor was the only player who would make it to the Majors.

For the 2000 draft, Chip and I were also talking with a player who decided not to have an advisor. The player told teams he would sign if drafted in the first 10 rounds. When he was drafted in the 7th round, he was offered $75,000 to sign and turned them down. We met with the family, and they wanted $200,000 to sign. We explained that when they told teams they would sign in the first 10 rounds, they were conveying they would take round money if drafted in any of those rounds. We advised them to contact the team and let them know they didn't intend to convey that, and it would take $200,000 to sign. Fortunately for the player, he continued to throw well during the summer, allowing the scouting director to see the player. He eventually signed for $175,000.

Although the player didn't sign with us, it confirmed Chip and I had learned the ropes and we knew what we were doing.

As I reflected on the year, I wrote in my journal.

11/3/00

As I look back over the year, I can clearly see God's hand at work. God has prepared me for the next step through failures. Now I'm more experienced, more prepared, better services offered. I have made myself more attractive to players. I wouldn't have made it to this point if I didn't have failures. (Failure is a real opportunity to see what's missing.)

CHAPTER 10

The Long Shot

> Trust in the Lord with all your heart and lean not on
> your own understanding; in all your ways acknowledge
> him, and he will make your paths straight.
>
> PROV. 3:5-6

As I continued to move forward with my dream, I never thought much about how great of a risk it was, or how slim the chance of success. I was simply focused on the task at hand, continuing to explore ways to move forward and pursue my career goals. I was constantly cutting overhead, and increasing revenue. One of those cuts involved Chip. It was an easy decision since I simply didn't have the funds to pay his salary anymore. Although he had been instrumental in helping me recruit Taylor, we both agreed that being my associate wasn't sustainable, and we mutually agreed to part ways. So I found myself back on my own, much further along than I would have been otherwise, but with a lot less money in my pocket.

On the revenue side, I continued to find ways to get positive exposure. The local paper had written an article on me. It had been a slow news day, so a photographer asked if he could come by my office and take a picture. The next day an article appeared about my agency breaking into the sports' industry and doing so with ethics. Since my neighbor worked at Channel 9 news, they also did a small feature. Just like my players, I was slowly moving up the ladder. At one point, I had read a feature article about baseball in the *Washington Post Magazine*, so I contacted the writer, Jim Naughton, and asked if he would do a story on me. Low and behold, he got approval from the Post and said yes. Jim was a freelance writer, but he had been a former beat writer with the Mets, and he contributed stories to the magazine. I told him he could follow me around and write whatever he wanted. I was convinced God was behind this, so I was willing to trust the article would glorify Him. I also believed the article was another sign from God, and He was telling me I was on the right path.

In May 2001, Jim tagged along to a college baseball tournament in New Jersey, where I went to watch a player I was advising in the upcoming draft. During the trip, we also traveled to see Taylor Buchholz pitch in Salisbury, Maryland. I must have spoken with 15 different scouts at the New Jersey tournament, and each one was very friendly to me. Unfortunately, when the story came out, the story focused on one particular encounter with a scout I spoke with, who didn't know me and wasn't very forthcoming with information.

As we continued to meet and go on short road trips to see my players and potential prospects, Jim envisioned the story being about the pursuit of a dream, and he clearly saw my commitment to living out my faith. But the magazine seemed to direct him toward making it seem like I had given up my law practice, and risked everything. Granted, my law practice had taken a hit, but I wasn't about to completely quit my day job, and it wasn't accurate to what was happening.

As Jim followed me around, I must have had five or six separate photography sessions with David Deal, a freelance photographer hired by the *Post*, who had published a book of photography of minor league players and ballparks throughout the country. He followed me to Salem, Virginia; Richmond, Virginia; and Hagerstown, Maryland, to photograph me with my players. He took pictures of me with my family at home, and with me talking to other lawyers at the courthouse. In each session, he must have taken a few hundred pictures. I felt like a celebrity. My fifteen minutes of fame had arrived. Meanwhile, Jim also interviewed Marie, who didn't share the same enthusiasm. But, on a positive note, she talked about how she had started a women's prayer and support group for husbands who owned their own business.

In Salem, VA Spring 2001

In our backyard, Spring 2001

The story was scheduled to be published in September 2001 but, with the tragedy of 9/11, the story was bumped until further notice. Baseball went into the off-season, and I pivoted my focus back on criminal defense.

I had already made plans to assist another attorney with his practice, so I tabled any future sports agency pursuits for the winter. I had hoped the article would give me a boost, and expose me to more prospects, so I was very disappointed, but I adapted and continued to trust God's timing.

The main source of stress was that I was working for someone else, which was hard for me because I liked the freedom of working for myself. But I was helping out more at home, and that was good for our marriage and our kids.

The following spring I received a call from Jim, who informed me the story was picked up again, and he was going to meet me in Florida during Spring Training. At the time, I was representing six players, with at least one prospect and one other potential prospect. I didn't see the story until it came out on May 26, 2002.

'The Long Shot – The Agent; what happens when you risk everything to follow your dream' was on the cover of the *Washington Post Magazine*. Because of the delay and, with the addition of the Spring Training trip, the article had become a feature story. It started with the most recent trip to Spring Training, as Jim and I watched a minor league game with Tim Hamulack. In the distance, we could hear the announcer shouting the lineup for the Major League Spring Training game between the Cardinals and Expos at Jupiter Stadium. Using that moment, the article stated,

Pasti is convinced that someday he'll hear the name of one of his clients drifting in amplified echo from a major league stadium...

The article immediately made me a local celebrity. It was a 12-page spread, with a picture of me with a client, Brandon Agamennone, on the cover. In some ways it was much more than I expected, but it certainly didn't portray me as a successful agent. Still, Jim did a good job showing how my faith directed my actions. I knew the article would appeal to people who shared similar values. I hoped it would appeal to the Christian athlete who was looking for an agent they could trust.

Picture with Taylor, Hagerstown, MD June, 2001

I asked the *Washington Post* for 150 copies, and mailed one to every contact I could think of. Over the previous four years I had made some good contacts in the baseball industry, including college and high school coaches, farm directors, scouts, members of the media, and a few general managers.

Although I couldn't quantify the success of the article, I received a call that was most encouraging, and it began a friendship, and later a partnership, that continued throughout my career. A fellow sports agent, Joe Kohm, was on a similar path, and appeared to be a few steps ahead. He was a former college basketball player at Syracuse, whose claim to fame was playing on the team that made it to the NCAA finals in 1987.

Joe was also a lawyer who felt he could use his gifts representing athletes. On that fall day in 2002, he called to encourage me. Even though he was technically my competition, he was also a Christian and told me to hang in there and continue to fight the good fight. He had a partner at the time, so he wasn't looking to work together. But God had other things in mind.

Joe and I continued to talk, and we eventually agreed to meet. From there, we agreed to go after a few top players together for the 2003 draft. Although we lost out on a few 1st and 2nd round players, we managed to represent the first five players chosen from the state of Maryland. I was fortunate to advise a little-known prospect out of Cumberland, Maryland, named Aaron Laffey. We also advised an 8th rounder, two 13th rounders, and a 34th round draft and follow.[4]

---

[4] Some teams take a player in the later rounds and follow him during the summer in the hopes of signing him before he attends college in the fall. More recently, the deadline to sign a player changed, and eliminated the draft and follow.

CHAPTER 11

Balancing Act

> You can make an analogy between their careers and mine in terms of working their way up. Of course, they don't have a wife and three children. Washington Post Magazine,
>
> MAY 26, 2002

After the *Post* article, I felt like I had to continue pursuing my dream. I mean, there I was on the cover of the *Washington Post Magazine*! I had come this far, and waited a year for the article to finally come out. I couldn't turn back now. However, Marie wasn't feeling the same way. Some of her concerns were expressed in the article: *Is this going to happen, and when is it going to happen?*

I didn't have an answer for her. Although she had been expressing her concerns, and they weren't a surprise, it was a bit discouraging to see them in print. At least I knew they were serious, and we needed to address them.

When it came to risks, the compromise we'd found early in our marriage was wearing thin. Marie continued to be very cautious regarding risks, and she knew that could often be a good thing. She helped me think through my ideas before acting on them. As long as I was willing to listen to her concerns, she would usually let me decide how to move forward. However, if she had strong feelings against moving forward, I had learned to stop without her blessing, or at least until her willingness to support my decision.

For me, people have called me many things, but no one has ever called me cautious. I am reminded of a quote attributed to a famous missionary, Hudson Taylor – "without an element of risk, there is no need for God." The real question for me was this. Was God directing me to continue the sports' agency? The answer for me was yes. Reluctantly, Marie went along with my assessment.

To bring in income, I continued to practice law, and I tried several ways to cut overhead. I tried working out of my home, helping another lawyer with his practice and, finally, I took a salary at a law firm so I could keep my dream alive. My law practice was getting fewer and fewer calls, that well was running dry.

But, despite the changes I made to bring stability and income, being a sports' agent continued to demand we take risks and make sacrifices. I continued spending time away from home as I traveled to watch baseball games. This caused additional stress for Marie, who was home with three very active boys. Marie's dream was to have the freedom to stay home full-time while the kids were little (or work only part-time), and mine was to be a sports' agent. Our dreams were in full course collision.

If I had known how long it would take to earn enough income from being an agent to support a family, I might not have pursued the dream in the first place. But I was naïve and optimistic. Not a good combination. The more I told my wife that it would take just one more year, the less she believed me. I was losing credibility as she had heard the same thing for the previous three years. I would have been better off telling her I didn't know how long it would take, and talking with her about how long she was willing to go.

But there came a point, in the beginning of 2003, when I knew I couldn't continue to move forward without Marie 100 percent behind me. We decided to get professional counseling so each of us could feel heard, as my wife would say. We also met with another couple who had faced similar issues.

Both the counselor, and the couple, seemed to support the idea of moving forward with the baseball agency, at least that's how I remember it. And Marie had a lightbulb moment, which helped us talk through the challenges and find a way forward. We had some money to fall back on, so we wouldn't be going into debt at this point by continuing the baseball business. We were also starting to communicate better.

2/18/03

Good conversation with Marie about the Spring baseball season. Started off bad, but we recovered. We are not far apart in how we will handle the Spring, still need to plan. I still need to try to bring in money, but she's okay with a little debt for the sake of the draft. But we do need to learn from our mistakes, according to Marie. But I can only do so much in the Spring to bring in money. I'm not willing to be tied down to a boss.

As we worked through the challenges, we recognized our kids had grown old enough for me to take them to games. By the spring of 2003, I was representing six players, and whenever a player was within driving distance, I tried to meet up with him. Brandon Agamennone was playing at the AA level with the Harrisburg Senators, about 90 minutes from our home. In the summer of 1999, I took my first overnight road trip with my boys, Jon and Michael. At ages six and four, it worked out for the most part, although it was difficult for them to sit still for the entire game. Usually, I bribed them with a souvenir and some ice cream, and we made it through. I was constantly trying to find new and creative ways to pursue the dream, and make it work for all of us.

Normally I would go out with the player after the game but, when the kids were young and traveling with me, I told the player I would be either leaving right after the game, or when they were done pitching.

Taking the kids to games made for some good bonding time with my boys, and it gave Marie a well-needed break. But the time away from home would continue to increase, something neither of us anticipated when we got married. Yet Frank Young's advice about when you're praying for direction stayed in the back of my mind. He advised not to focus too much on time away from home. (Although now that advice could be a bit outdated.) I headed down to Spring Training in Florida for four days in early March, then back home for a few days before flying to Arizona for three days. While in Arizona, I journaled, recognizing the opportunity God was opening for me as I balanced my marriage and family.

3/16/03

Going with the flow as the rain came. Ran into Mark Hagen (Matt Hagen's dad). Good talk to start the day, then to church service to get priorities in place. Call to Marie to apologize. Opportunity knocks – ran into Tim Kurkjian (from ESPN – Mike Toomey had introduced me to him at the Winter Meetings and he lives in the DC Metro Area). Good conversation with him; then found out the Tim Hamulack was sent down. Then conversation with Mike Toomey – Tim is marginal – I took it in stride as each day brings ups and downs. Not sure what the next step is, but I am finally getting close to letting go completely. It's in God's hands. He will show me the next step. I don't have to force it. It brings great comfort and relief as well as excitement as to where God will lead me, but I do get excited when I see how my faith can be expressed in baseball. Perhaps I need to be a bit more outspoken. Marie and I could be a good example to these young players.

CHAPTER 12

Aaron Laffey

Never surrender opportunity for security.

BRANCH RICKEY

Aaron Laffey was a little-known, left-handed pitcher from Cumberland, Maryland, a small city in rural Western Maryland. I had received a tip from a college coach in the fall of 2002 about him. He was 6 feet tall, and barely 160 lbs., but he was a very polished pitcher for his age. Aaron's father grew up with Leo Mazzone, so he had been priming Aaron since he was five years old. I contacted the family, and Aaron's mother had seen the article in the *Post* about me. She told me she was a Christian, and she immediately seemed comfortable with me. She would later tell me I was an answer to her prayers.

Initially the Laffey family didn't know if they needed an advisor. Although several teams had met with them during the winter, they weren't contacted by any other advisors, so I was also unsure if they needed me. I followed up with them, and asked if I could to come up to watch Aaron play basketball. I had talked with several scouts who told me they found out a lot about a player when they saw him playing another sport.

Immediately I could tell Aaron was a competitor. He was the starting point guard for Alleghany High School, a 1-A school with about 800 students. Aaron played with a lot of emotion, but it was a controlled emotion. After the game, I spoke with Aaron for a few minutes and met his mother, father, and Aaron's girlfriend, Jackie (his future wife).

Once baseball season started, I went up to watch Aaron pitch. In his first game, he threw a perfect game for five innings, and only one player managed to put the ball in play. The game was called due to the mercy rule. Aaron was better than advertised, and I was convinced I could help him. But it wasn't a done deal.

3/24/03
The ups and downs continue to test my faith, as it has been mostly downs. Even the excitement about Laffey with 15 scouts quickly soured as the parents are going to wait. My faith is being tested on a daily basis. Don't let the circumstances dictate my faith.

I continued to talk with Mrs. Laffey and, in mid-April, she told me if they went with anyone, it would be me. With each passing start, the pressure continued to mount for the Laffey family. Several scouts and cross-checkers were coming to games, and beginning to ask the Laffeys for a number – what it would take for Aaron to sign. Finally, Mrs. Laffey called to say they could use my assistance, and I went to their home to meet. We talked for three and half hours and, in the end, Aaron knew what signing bonus he would be willing to accept to sign with a team.

I was clear, or I thought I was clear, as I explained the difference between what the teams think he's worth versus what he and his family thought. A team is not simply going to give a player what they're asking for. Aaron knew that once he told teams what it would take, some teams would no longer be interested. The pie would get smaller. But I wasn't certain about what Aaron would do if no teams were interested in him, after we told teams what it would take to sign. He could simply go to Virginia Tech, where a full scholarship was waiting for him. Still, it was time to give the teams a number. Instead of saying an exact number, we told them Aaron needed to be drafted in the first 75 picks. Pick number 75 was projected to be $500,000.

Four days later, on May 13, 2003, I observed the best high school game I'd ever seen. Alleghany's opponent was Williamsport in the Maryland Class 1A quarterfinals. Aaron faced off against Nick Adenhart, a junior, who was already a top prospect topping out at 94 MPH. These two pitchers were clearly the two best pitchers in the state of Maryland. It seemed like half the town of Cumberland was there to witness a piece of high school baseball history.

The game lived up to its expectations. Aaron had nineteen strikeouts, and allowed two hits. Nick had fourteen strikeouts and pitched a no hitter. Alleghany won 1-0 on a hit by pitch, stolen base, and a squeeze bunt. There were fourteen Major League scouts in attendance. Aaron earned some money that day. I remember thinking that someday, the two of them could pitch against each other in a Major League game[5].

---

[5] Unfortunately, in April 2010, Nick Adenhart died after being hit by a drunk driver who ran a stop sign. Both Aaron and Nick were in the Majors at the time.

The game against Williamsport would be the last time Aaron pitched at this level so, unless Aaron was invited to a pre-draft workout, he wouldn't be seen again before the draft. During this time, I was also advising another left-handed pitcher, Joe Wilson, who was a junior at the University of Maryland at Baltimore County (UMBC). Joe was another guy who was under the radar. Unfortunately, prior to one of his last games, he was hit on the head with a baseball in the outfield during batting practice, and put on the injury list.

As Joe recovered, teams asked about his health. Since his season was over as well, there wasn't an opportunity for scouts to see him pitch and assess his physical condition. So I had to create an opportunity for both Joe and Aaron. I noticed the upcoming ACC baseball tournament was in Salem, Virginia, and I had made a few contacts down there when I attended the Virginia Commonwealth Games the previous year.

I made arrangements for Aaron, Joe, and a few other pitchers, to pitch at an old Minor league stadium down the street from where the ACC tournament was being held. I knew each Major League team would have at least one scout in attendance, so I arranged a time when no teams were playing, and then spread the word to the scouts. Unfortunately, the rain came and they didn't let us use the field. I quickly had to come up with plan B, which I hadn't planned for in advance.

I spoke with my contact, and he told me about an indoor facility a few miles away. I persuaded them to open it for us, and we spread the word to the scouts about the change in plans. In the scouting world, news travels fast. There's definitely a cow herd mentality. A scout doesn't want to miss an opportunity for fear that his supervisor will ask him why he didn't see a particular pitcher who was drafted by another team. Most scouts will share information with other scouts about when someone is pitching, with the hope they will return the favor.

With the heavy rain coming down, my little showcase was the only show in town. At least twenty scouts showed up – standing room only. In fact, there was only enough room for one or two people to stand behind the catcher, so one scout shouted out the velocity after each pitch. The event was a great success, especially since there were at least a few scouting directors in attendance and both Joe[6] and Aaron performed well.

5/21/03

One of the most satisfying days of an agent ever! Somehow I knew things would work out with the workout, even though it rained. It took God's intervention, as options were running out and we had to move fast while scouts were available. Once we found an alternate place, I was on the phone calling the scouts – we had a great turnout – 20 scouts!

Aaron had finished the season with some incredible statistics. He didn't allow an earned run all season! In other words, he had a 0.00 ERA in 44.1 innings pitched. He allowed nine hits and eight walks, and had 116 strikeouts out – of a total of 133 outs.

As draft day approached, teams were calling about Aaron's signability. After talking with the interested teams, there appeared to be only three to four teams considering him in those first 75 picks. The night before the draft, the Braves called to tell Aaron the amount they were giving for their picks. The Braves had a few extra picks in the early rounds. The most relevant picks to us were pick #68 at $525,000 and pick #79 at $450,000. Aaron said he would sign for $450,000 if they picked him at pick #79.

---

[6] Joe Wilson was drafted by the Phillies in the 13th round.

I knew the Braves are one of the only teams to use this approach, and they stick with their number. Many teams are willing to go above the slot to sign a player, that's why it's usually better to give an amount rather than a round. I had learned this by looking at the draft results in previous years, and there were always players who signed above round money. I was ready to help the Laffey family negotiate.

During the draft I decided to be at the Laffey home in case something unexpected came up, as it usually does. Every year, teams call players during the draft to see if a player will take a certain amount to sign, especially when the player doesn't get drafted where they were expecting. As the draft began over the internet, and we listened to each name being called, anxiety increased. The draft moves very quickly, with a name being called out every ten seconds. It didn't take long to get through the first 75 picks, and we still had not heard Aaron's name. Perhaps Aaron really did want to sign, and was asking for too much. Certainly, he believed he was worth $500,000, but it was becoming more apparent the teams didn't value him that high.

I knew several teams would still take players in later rounds, and pay in the $500,000 range. So, we had made it clear that Aaron didn't have to get picked in the first 75 picks, but he was clear about what it would take to sign. Finally, the Braves called right after their pick #79 and asked if Aaron would sign if they took him with their next pick at pick #95. That amount was $395,000. After a quick conversation, Aaron said he would take it.

We anxiously waited for the next few minutes to hear Aaron's name and, when it was the Braves turn, the Braves' representative called out, "Matt Harrision, left-handed pitcher…" Wow, we were all stunned. We assumed the Braves would take Aaron after they took the time to call. Unfortunately, they didn't anticipate that Matt Harrison would still be on the board.

I told Aaron to hold his ground, and not go below that amount. I knew other teams could call and ask him if he would take a certain amount to sign, and that amount would be significantly lower than his asking price. I assured him a team would still draft him in the later rounds, and try to sign him. I decided to head back home to my family, a couple hours away.

Later that day, the Cleveland Indians drafted Aaron in the 16th round. They immediately called Aaron to tell him they wanted to sign him. Although no figure was mentioned, their interest was sincere. Since Aaron was scheduled to pitch in a college summer league, the Indians wanted their scouting director to see Aaron before making an offer.

A week later Aaron was back on the mound, but only with the area scout for the Indians in attendance. He wanted to make sure Aaron was pitching well before bringing in the scouting director. He also made clear we weren't talking about the first 75 picks anymore. Aaron had another good outing, and the scout assured us the scouting director would attend the next game. The next game was rained out, so finally on June 23, Aaron had an opportunity to earn some money. He didn't disappoint. We were told an offer would be forthcoming in 24 to 48 hours.

The Indians came back with an offer of $300,000, very close to what I expected. Teams will not pay a penny more than they have to, so they always start out low. Also, they had the draft on their side, since 29 other teams passed on Aaron. They also believed Aaron wanted to sign, so they had some leverage. Aaron was certainly willing to be flexible, and he understood he may have overvalued himself. I probably would have talked him down if I thought he really didn't want to go to college. But he had convinced me that if he didn't get what he wanted, he would go to Virginia Tech.

After seeing how disappointed he was in not getting drafted higher, and then how excited he was when the Indians told him they wanted to sign him, I was convinced Aaron really wanted to sign. But we still had leverage, and I needed Aaron and his family to be patient in the negotiation process.

We decided to come back with $450,000, probably a bit on the high side, but at least a starting point in the negotiations. However, the Indians didn't make another offer. They wanted us to make another offer that didn't have a 4 in it, or else they wouldn't go any further in the negotiations. So we came back with $399,500. They came back with $350,000. I shared our experience we had with the Braves, and suggested that Aaron was worth $395,000. We finally agreed on $363,000, and Aaron signed his first professional contract. The deal earned me a fee of $10,890 (3%). The Laffeys had full faith and confidence in me, and I'd gone to battle for them.

After reporting to the Indians spring training facility in Winter Haven, Florida, Aaron was assigned to their rookie level in Burlington, North Carolina, in the Appalachian league, only four levels before the Majors! His debut was on July 9, 2003, in Princeton, West Virginia. I saw him pitch two innings, no hits. He had a lot of confidence.

What stood out for me in his debut was the fact he called off the catcher's signal for a fastball on a 3-2 count, and struck out the batter with a breaking ball. That's moxie, and that's what the Indians saw in drafting him.

In the end, especially with high school players, I found it was better to err on the high side in deciding a signing bonus amount in most cases. A player can always come off his figure. For college players, it's better to make them as signable as possible, and have more teams in the pie. Still, there are many high school players who turn down hundreds of thousands of dollars to attend college and then, three years later, sign for a lot more. I knew Aaron could have been one of those players, but he was eager to start his career.

And as someone pursuing my dream, I couldn't blame him.

CHAPTER 13

Minor League Agent

> When it comes to success, there are no shortcuts.
>
> BO BENNETT

You have to crawl before you walk. That's what I've been told. In the baseball world, with a few exceptions, the crawling is the minor leagues. The same goes for the agent. Since the player is only making $1,000 to $2,000 per month, the agent doesn't earn any income. Not until I had a player reach the Majors would I be considered anything but a minor league agent. It is certainly a humbling title, and a blow to the ego, but sometimes that is how the truth works. For my first seven years as an agent, I didn't step foot into a Major League stadium, except as an occasional spectator.

I knew I would have to start somewhere, and that somewhere was the bottom. But I did find some positives. Representing minor league players meant I could begin to include my family. Marie was also seeing the positives, as I continued taking the boys to games with me, and it expanded their horizons as they got older. I also got to travel and see many new places. I traveled to most minor league ballparks on the East coast, and watched games at every level, from rookie ball to AAA, and everything in between. I saw where the Muckdogs and Mudcats play, and I watched the Smokies, Battle Caps, Renegades, BlueClaws, Intimidators, Grasshoppers, Sand Gnats, Express, Sea Dogs and Bisons, just to name a few.

I even attended many independent ball games in the Atlantic League and Can-Am League. That's where players go to play after they get released from affiliated ball. Places like Lancaster, Pennsylvania, and Waldorf, Maryland, or Somerset, New Jersey. That's where an agent really earns his wings – if he takes on a player from independent ball, and the player makes it to the Majors.

I enjoyed taking my sons to games with me, one at a time. My first son to join me on a trip was Jonny in 2003 when he was 10 years old. We traveled to Michigan to visit Matt Hagen, who was playing Low-A ball in the Midwest league. Matt was the first player I represented who said he wanted a Christian agent. I had developed a relationship with the baseball coach at Liberty, back in 1999, so I would periodically check in with him about players, and he told me about Matt. I had reached out to Matt before the 2002 season. Matt was a committed Christian from an incredible family from Colorado. He was drafted in the 12th round of the 2002 draft as a junior out of Liberty University, and received a signing bonus of $38,000.

Traveling back to Michigan was also going back in time for me, as our family went to Lake Michigan to my grandfather's cabin several times in my childhood.

With my parents at Lake Michigan, Summer 1963

We tracked down the cabin, and it brought back a lot of good memories. It was one of the few times in my childhood where I felt at peace. My uncle sold the cabin in the early 80s, so I hadn't returned since 1976. Jonny and I also visited the Kellogg's plant, and climbed Mt Baldy in Saugatuck, Michigan. We swam in Lake Michigan, and watched Matt play in Battle Creek. Time away allowed me more opportunities to reflect and gain spiritual insight.

8/27/03

Great start to the day with reading the Bible. Gained some insight to relieve a lot of anxiety. The word of God hit me, focusing on Christ as our main goal. Before that had scared me; now it relieves me, gives me purpose and opportunity to make each day more fulfilling. I see today with a new perspective – an opportunity to live out my faith.

Also in 2003, our family traveled to Tennessee to visit my wife's relatives. Of course, we stopped on the way to see a player, Matt Foster, in Princeton, West Virginia. As I explained to my wife, if we could combine business and pleasure, we could write off at least some of the expenses. Unfortunately, that information didn't cause her to jump for joy, but she continued to be supportive. It was while we were in Princeton that our children began to get involved in the between-innings contests. We discovered that if we found the right person before a game, they could sign up to participate. The kids competed in a lot of dizzy bat, and run-the-bases contests, over the years. Although our boys had no idea I wasn't making much money as an agent, or understood the stress Marie and I felt, they enjoyed going to new places and being together as a family.

Matt Foster was the first player ever drafted out of the Naval Academy. He was drafted in the 13th round in the 2003 draft and allowed to play that summer, and then he had to fulfill his two-year commitment to the Navy. Because our country was at war in Afghanistan, the Navy would not waive his commitment. Since then, there have been other players drafted from other branches of the military, and those branches have allowed the players to play. The game in Princeton was the only game I ever saw Matt play. A couple years after his tour, he tried to play again, but without success. During the two-year period, I had lost contact with him, and found out later that he chose one of his friends to become his agent. However, by then, he wasn't considered a prospect.

Later in the summer of 2003 I took my 7-year-old son, Michael, on a train trip to Beacon, New York, to visit my older sister and watch the Batavia Muckdogs play the Hudson Valley Renegades. Michael was a train enthusiast and, since it was hard for him to sit still at his age, it was great to have the freedom of walking throughout the train. We stopped briefly in New York City, and then we headed north on the Hudson Line from

Grand Central Station. We enjoyed spending time with my older sister, who lived in Beacon, just five minutes away from the stadium.

It was the first of many trips to Hudson Valley to see various players. On this occasion, we went to see Marc Tugwell, the son of the legendary high school coach at West Springfield High School, Ron Tugwell. I had met Coach Tugwell when I first started in 1998, when his son was still in high school. Marc went on to have a great college career at Virginia Tech, where he batted over .400 his senior year. Still, he wasn't drafted until the 22nd in the 2003 draft, as he didn't have any exceptional tools, but he played the game well. Marc made it to Hi-A over the next few years, but also topped out as most organizational players do at that level.

I tried to take my three-year-old son, Sammy, on an overnight trip. We planned to drive to Lancaster, Pennsylvania, in the afternoon, and stay overnight. Then we attended a game the next day in Reading, and see Taylor Buchholz pitch in an AA game. Unfortunately, the temperature was 100 degrees at game time, so Sammy lasted only three innings before he started to melt down. I wasn't up for the battle. But attempting to take Sammy to a game gave Marie a little break, and it gave her some time with just the older boys. Taking our youngest was helpful, since our older two boys were age eight and ten, and could entertain themselves most of the time.

There were minor league games and independent ball, and there were also summer college baseball wooden bat leagues. Since the colleges still use aluminum bats during the season, the summer leagues presented a good opportunity for prospects to be seen by scouts using wood bats. The most prestigious summer league is the Cape Cod League. The top college players in the draft are mostly from that league and, of course, that's where most agents are as well.

I joined the masses in 2003, and went to the Cape in search of a prospect. I mainly focused on players who were from the Mid-Atlantic region, and tried to make contact before they left for the summer. I met with several players, and ended up being there during my final negotiations with the Indians on Aaron Laffey. By the time I left the Cape, the deal with Aaron Laffey was done, and I landed one prospect for the 2004 draft.

In the midst of all the traveling and excitement, the reality was hard. I wasn't making much money. Thankfully, Marie was willing to consider going back to work. If this dream of mine was really part of God's plan, both of us needed to do our part. There was a lot going on inside the Pasti home.

8/27/03

The money just stopped coming in – But Marie did initiate her willingness to work, but it takes a lot of discussion about child care, etc.

9/1/03

Marie and I did have a productive conversation about her working – I said it would help our relationship – less resentment; extra money; begin her career.

11/7/03

Marie is able to begin working – starting out with Monday and Tuesday evenings; and Wednesday and Friday mornings – that's about $500 per month.

I recognized I also needed to do my part so, in the fall of 2003, I accepted a temporary full-time job with another attorney that would take me to the spring of 2004.

CHAPTER 14

Hitting Bottom

> We also exult in our tribulations, knowing that tribulation brings about perseverance; and perseverance, proven character; and proven character, hope; and hope does not disappoint, because the love of God has been poured out within our hearts through the Holy Spirit who was given to us.
>
> ROMANS 5:3-5

As the 2003 season came to an end, I finally had a few major league prospects. Tim Hamulack had become a minor league free agent, and I was able to negotiate for his services with several teams. Tim had finished his seventh year in the minors, and he had a very good year at AA. No one aspires to be a minor league free agent, but when that happens, a player is no longer obligated to the team that drafted him. He can sign with any team, and he can begin to earn a living making anywhere from $8,000 to $15,000 per month during the five-month minor league season.

Fortunately, at least 15 teams called to inquire about Tim's services. It was realistic for Tim to get a coveted spot on the 40-man roster, and that also meant I could be certified with the Player's Association, the union for the Major League players. Having a player reach this level was basically a rite of passage for an agent. It would allow me to attend the annual mandatory meetings for all certified agents in New York, Chicago, or Los Angeles. It also helped with recruiting players – if you could say you were a certified agent, it gave you more credibility.

The Red Sox had seen Tim pitch in Puerto Rico during winter ball, and clocked him as high as 94 MPH. They wanted him enough to offer him a Major League contract. After five years of being an agent, I had a real boost to my career. At the annual meeting in November, I found myself in the same room with agents like Rex Gary, Michale Moye, and Michael Maas who worked with Ron Shapiro. All of them were very friendly, and willing to give me advice. But there were many other agents there who wouldn't think twice about trying to go after other agents' players.

About the same time, Taylor Buchholz was traded to the Astros in the Billy Wagner trade, and was soon ranked the Number 1 prospect in the Astros organization by *Baseball America*. Since Taylor had completed his 4th season, the Astros needed to either place him on the 40-man roster, or risk losing him to the Rule 5 draft. He was my second player to be added to the 40-man roster. Aaron Laffey had made a good start with his professional career after signing in July, and he was also a Major League prospect. Matt Hagen had some serious raw power at 6ft 5 and 220 lbs. He hit 21 home runs in Low A ball, and made the Midwest League All-Star team.

As thrilled as I was about the players' success, I was also learning it's one thing to have players, but it's another thing to keep players. Over the years, I had met lots of aspiring baseball agents, and we all had one thing in common – the experience of losing players to bigger agencies. Many agents are always approaching players to entice them to change agents; and it doesn't matter if a player already has an agent. I was fortunate that both Tim and

Taylor chose to stick with me. I can honestly say that I've never tried to take a player away from another agent. Perhaps, as a lawyer, I have a different mentality. The law profession has professional rules of conduct, and it is unethical to pursue a potential client who is represented by another lawyer. It's like taking food off someone's table. Agents don't have the same code of ethics.

As I secured a few players for the 2004 draft, one of them let me know about another agent who told him I blew a big deal, and the agent said he was making a big mistake by going with me. Certainly, it was a legitimate sales tactic if it was true, but I hadn't blown a big deal. Sure, Aaron Laffey didn't sign for what he initially asked for, but he signed for a good amount, and things worked out for him. If this agent was spreading misinformation, I knew it was slander, and he could be held civilly liable. I got on the phone with the agent, and asked if he had said I blew a big deal. He said yes. But when I asked what deal he was talking about, he said he didn't know, he was repeating what he had heard. I was even more disturbed at his recklessness, not even willing to check the accuracy of the information he was sharing. I made sure he knew I was a lawyer, and I explained he could be civilly liable for what he said. I followed up with a letter and, fortunately for him, that was the last time I heard about it.

In spring 2004, both Taylor and Tim were at a Major League camp for the first time! But there were still about 60 players there, and only 25 make the Major League roster. Taylor wasn't expecting to make the big-league club, but Tim had an outside chance. The excitement continued to build with each passing day that Tim remained at camp. I would call one of the assistant GMs so regularly, it prompted him to comment that I was calling a lot. Tim continued to pitch well, compiling a respectable 2.23 ERA. It came down to the last day of spring training, and Tim was the last guy to get cut. The dreaded 26th man.

Teams can only have 25 men on their active roster. The rest of the 40-man roster is optioned to either AAA or AA. Unless you're a veteran, or you had a good year in the Majors the previous year, it is very difficult to make the team out of spring training. There are also a few players who are out of options, so they also have a better chance of making the team. (Before they can be sent down, they have to clear waivers, and any other team can claim them and put them on their 40-man roster.) Still, guys are being called up to the Majors on a regular basis, so Tim had a chance to be the next guy up.

Unfortunately, Tim didn't take the news well. He had worked so hard, and pitched so well during spring training, and still didn't make it. I tried to keep his hopes up. After all, the average team uses at least 40 players during a season. As expected, the lefty who beat out Tim for the last spot, only lasted a week in the Majors. But Tim was passed over for another lefty, and that only deepened the wound. He never recovered, and it showed with his pitching. He was eventually taken off the 40-man roster and finished the season with a 6.98 ERA.

Meanwhile, Taylor and Aaron continued to pitch well. By August, Taylor was a candidate to be called up but, in August, he was shut down with an impingement in his shoulder. Aaron started out at the lower levels. Although he took a brief step back to rookie ball, he rebounded and finished the season in Low A ball.

I headed back up to Cape, this time with my family, and another family from our church who had four boys. That meant we had seven boys in the same house, ranging from age three to age 12! They were planning to go to Cape Cod for vacation, so we decided to share a home with them. Between the four adults, we were able to keep the boys busy, and we also took turns so each couple could spend time away from the kids. It was also convenient to be in the same area where some of my prospects were playing.

I had secured two top prospects for the 2005 draft, so I wanted to see them play and protect them from other agents. Marie knew how important it was for me to see these players, so she didn't complain when I left the house to watch games. I attended a game every night with at least two of the boys, and I usually took the kids somewhere during the day. The children had a great time, but I knew my wife was relieved when we got back to our house. Truth be told, I was too. The success of Tim and Taylor felt fleeting, and we were being dealt a lot of blows.

7/2/04

My attitude took a turn for the worse when Joe told me that Jeremy Griffiths was called up – another big blow. I took it hard, unable to be in a good mood. It came to the surface when we got stuck in a huge traffic backup. Told Marie it's how I feel now – stuck – I need something to give me hope.

Taylor had been performing well at AAA, but was also passed over. There was a looming question about Matt Hagen – could he handle the more advanced pitchers? The answer was no. He hit only nine home runs in Hi-A and, in his second year at Hi-A in 2005, he only batted .185. That was the beginning of the end of his career in affiliated ball.[7]

While at the Cape, I sensed that one of my players was acting a little more distant, which usually means he's talking with other agents. I decided to return to the Cape a month later to confirm either way. I took my son, Jonny, and we had a great time. He was up for anything, so he didn't mind when we spent all day at the Cape Cod All-Star game. But my intuition

---

[7] He played independent ball in 2005, and then from 2007-2012.

was correct, and the player told me he decided to go with another agency. The pressure from other agents was too much, and I didn't do enough to establish a good relationship with him.

8/12/04

Not able to have any joy lately. Stuck in feeling sick, not knowing when I'll get better; no exercise; and no further certainty as to when I'll make it in baseball. So taking more law cases. Thought: perhaps God hasn't allowed a player to make it because I need to take the same road as players so I can offer encouragement to others.

I still had Mike Costanzo, who was from the same area as Taylor. Taylor's dad had given Mike's father a ringing endorsement for me, so they decided to have me as his advisor in the middle of his sophomore year. Mike participated in the Home Run Derby at the Cape Cod League All-Star game and, by the end of the summer, he was one of the top 30 prospects in the league. More importantly, I was still his advisor!

But by the end of the 2004 season, I still didn't have any players in the Majors. That had been my ultimate dream, and goal. Mentally, I reached my lowest point, and I was beginning to question if God wanted me to continue pursuing my dream. There was no way to know if, and when, I would begin to earn enough income as an agent. If I had an endless supply of money, it wouldn't have been a problem, but our savings were quickly decreasing, and I knew funds would eventually run out in only a few years. I had also resorted to borrowing money using a credit line, and that was increasing quickly.

I have never been a person who stays down for long. Perhaps that's because of my childhood. But I have always found something to help change my focus, or give me new perspective. In the fall of 2004, I had an opportunity to be the head coach of Jon's baseball team. I had always been too busy in the spring, but I was usually home in the fall. This coaching opportunity was just what I needed, and the experience was much more than I could have expected.

Having focused on the business of baseball for the previous six years, I was wound up tight. I needed something to loosen me up, and take my mind off the constant pressures. Sure, my career was on the line, but my life still needed to be lived. As a Christian, that meant more than just my career. I was committed to living out my faith daily, so my attitude in the midst of the storm was important for those around me to see.

I happened to get a great group of kids to coach. That helped, but what I didn't know was there was another team that usually won every year, and we weren't expected to win. But something started to happen after the first few games – we were winning. I was finding something I had been missing. I was enjoying baseball again. I was allowing most kids to pitch, and play different positions, something most coaches wouldn't do. I continued to encourage them, rather than put them down, and I even had one of my minor league players come out and give them some tips about hitting.

We faced the unbeatable team three times, and beat them every time. We went on to win the league championship 15 to 3. God used the experience to change my depressed attitude. I was re-energized and ready for another baseball season.

> *10/30/04*
>
> *Monumental Day! Won championship 15-3 – scored 6 runs in consecutive innings to pull away – another team effort. It was close for the first 3 innings. God gave me a gift of success. I needed it! Could not have written a better script.*

A few weeks prior, I had begun reading *The Purpose Driven Life* by Rick Warren. A popular bestseller, it took readers through a 40-day spiritual journey with a daily question prompting contemplation about why we're here on earth. For example, writing in my journal on September 15, I said: *Day one – In spite of all the advertising around me, how can I remind myself that life is really about living for God, not myself? – fill up on the word of God – daily.*

I began to fill up on the word of God and look for my purpose in opportunities presented to me, like coaching my son and his teammates. It began to help me get unstuck. By the end of the year, I was ready for a fresh start.

> *12/31/04*
>
> *I'm thankful this year is over! Time for a fresh start – looking forward to what God has in mind for 2005! Will I finally have a player in the Majors? Will I make enough baseball income to cover expenses? Will Marie earn more income? Will our marriage be better? Will I be able to cut down on practicing law? Will I move closer to God? Will I give it all to God? Will our kids grow in their faith?*

Most of those questions would be answered in the following year.

CHAPTER 15

Finally: A Major League Rep

And we know that God causes all things to work together for good to those who love God, to those who are called according to his purpose.

ROMANS 8:28

Tim Hamulack had finished the 2004 season in pain. I had a contact in Northern Virginia who worked with baseball players, and he recommended a doctor. I went along with Tim to meet the doctor, who found some bone chips in Tim's elbow. It was good news to learn the source of his pain, and it was easily repaired.

Tim was a free agent again, and signed with the New York Mets. Although he didn't get an offer for the 40-man, and he didn't get invited to Major League spring training, for the first time in a while Tim was not in pain. Taylor was back in Major League camp with the Astros, and Aaron was ready for the next level.

The 2005 season was filled with excitement and stress. I knew I needed to make sure Marie was on board with my plans for the spring. Marie was enjoying a part-time job in Social Work, and was not planning to work full-time. We had a long talk, and prayed about it, before coming to an agreement.

2/10/05

Good conversation with Marie about finances and long-term goals – we will continue to pray, but focus is on the now. I'm going to go full out this Spring with baseball – still need to pray about investors; Marie is on board – going to support me.

I was advising Mike Costanzo, hoping he would be drafted high, so I put a lot of time and energy on him. He attended Coastal Carolina University in Myrtle Beach, so it was great to head south in February to start the season. I took my family for the first weekend tournament.

2/18/05

Fortunately we were able to get on the road by 6 am – smooth trip – only one skirmish with Sammy – Marie and I connected along the way – and that helped to set the tone – once we arrived, I went straight to the game – it was awesome – Mike went 4 for 5 HR, 4 RBI's – talked with lots of scouts – and reconnected with the Costanzos, and back to the hotel – the kids were tired, but had a good time. Fortunately all the kids were asleep by 9 pm. Marie feels good – that's a successful day.

I had also begun taking video of the players I was advising. A few years earlier I had been asked by a scout if I had some video of a player, so I figured if I was going to the game anyway, I might as well capture some footage. I even went a step further by putting music to the video, and a swing or windup in slow motion for emphasis.

Mike Costanzo was a two-way player, which meant teams were considering drafting him as a pitcher or as a hitter. He was closing games for Coastal Carolina, and playing 1st base. When Coastal's 3rd baseman went down with an injury, Mike took over at 3rd base and, according to a few scouts, Mike moved up a few rounds in the draft as he was able to show some versatility.

At the same time all of this was happening, lack of finances once again caused Marie and I stress. We had agreed I would go full out in the spring with baseball, but bills still needed to be paid. I continued to juggle two jobs; a baseball agent and a solo practice, focusing on personal injury and other cases. Going into the draft for the upcoming baseball season, I felt just as much pressure as the players, but for different reasons.

3/4/05

Finally heard back from State Farm – asked for a few more items – the moment of truth is near – this personal injury case, if settled, would provide me with necessary funding for the Spring – otherwise things don't look good, financially. Still, it's worth the risk for the draft.

> *3/5/05*
>
> *March 5 – Finally a day to relax – great walk on the beach – and ran for 12 minutes – 6 min against the wind – thought about analogy with how life has been, and reminded me of Bob Seger's song. We all need to run against the wind if we're going to get anywhere.*

> *5/15/05*
>
> *All doors have closed for income – investors; law cases; personal injury case; only hope is the draft – so I better be prepared for handling the draft.*

During a two-month span in the spring, I traveled to Myrtle Beach several times. In addition, I traveled to Georgia Tech in Atlanta, Winthrop in Rock Hill, South Carolina, and Elon and High Point in North Carolina. I put together quite a highlight reel of Mike's towering home runs, which included a shot off the lights at Winthrop. That shot was probably the longest ball ever hit there. Those in attendance included the scouting director of the Oakland A's, so Mike's stock was increasing as the season came to the close. At the Big South tournament the following week, the Phillies' scouting director was there, and saw Mike perform well.

FINALLY: A MAJOR LEAGUE REP

5/10/05

Off to Atlanta at 5:30 am to see Costanzo play at Georgia Tech. He rose to the occasion. About 15 scouts – talked with most of them – Padres scout was most helpful – told me where he had Mike – Group 1 as a Pitcher; Group 2 – hitter (Rounds 4/5).

I advised Mike to tell teams he was willing to go in the first 10 rounds, which meant he would take round money in any of those rounds. We wanted to make sure every team remained in the pie. But it also meant he would accept the slotted amount for that pick. We also told teams he wanted to be drafted as a hitter, as Mike was the type of player who liked to play every day and, except for the Padres, his stock as a hitter was much higher anyway.

The night before the draft, Mike was called by his hometown team, the Philadelphia Phillies. They told him if he was still available at pick #65 they would draft him. That was the Phillies' first pick in the 2005 draft since they had given up their first round pick by signing Jon Lieber in the offseason. When pick #65 was announced, I heard Mike's name. I jumped for joy and cried. They told Mike there would be a press conference in the evening prior to the Phillies game, and so I immediately got in my car and headed to Philly.

Upon arriving, I met and hugged Mike. I had developed a great relationship with him and his family, and he wanted me to share the experience with him. We were escorted through the locker room by Ed Wade, the GM. He introduced Mike to Jim Thome and Billy Wagner. It was a surreal experience. Agents are usually not allowed in the locker room at any time, especially before a game, but there are exceptions.

We headed back to Mike's parent's house, and were met by 100 family and friends. The Phillies asked if we could begin negotiating, so they came over as well. It certainly didn't help our leverage to negotiate at the same time and place where everyone was celebrating. However, both sides knew Mike would accept the slotted amount, so we just needed to agree. A deal was finally struck when the Phillies agreed to allow Mike to take batting practice with the team the next day. Mike signed the contract at around 3 am for a signing bonus of $565,000.

In the meantime, Tim Hamulack was quietly having the best year of his career. He had established a good relationship with his pitching coach, Dan Warthen, and that seemed to help. Tim was always extremely quiet to the point that some pitching coaches thought he didn't care. But Coach Warthen knew Tim was a fighter, and he was okay that Tim didn't talk much. But we would have to wait and see how things played out.

After the draft, it was back to reality. I had earned about $20,000 from Mike's signing bonus, but that money wouldn't come until later[8]. The next couple of months provided the usual ups and downs.

7/9/05

Met up with Tim H – it was exactly one year ago when I saw him at his low point – this year we're both doing better. Still waiting and hoping, but this time it feels different – like it's going to happen.

---

[8] Mike would get half of his bonus in six weeks, then the other half by January 31, 2006.

7/12/05

Listened to a Pastor Hicks on TV – talked about patience – God is helping to develop our faith – It may take years to see God's blessings – I can relate.

7/25/05

Back to the grindstone – sometimes it's the same old things with baseball – disappointments, injuries, problems, etc and waiting for something good to happen. And not much time to build baseball practice – it's hard to put in a full day of work with all my other obligations.

7/27/05

Still waiting on Tim H – it could be any day. ERA is down to .78

8/11/05

Dear God, the lack of cash flow has got me again – I am willing to submit, but I don't know what to do. I will continue to pray – at least I heard back from Taylor B, but he may not pitch for the rest of the season.

> *8/16/05*
>
> *With each passing day I seem to get more anxious about the future, especially when the phone doesn't ring much and I'm not feeling as if I'm moving forward. Although I'm putting things in God's hand, I need to have Tim make it – otherwise another season would go by without much change from last year with current players.*

I knew the Major League rosters were going to expand from 25 to 40 on September 1, and I was hopeful Tim would be called up, even though he wasn't on the 40-man roster. The Mets' roster at that time was under 40, so putting Tim on wouldn't mean taking someone off.

But out of nowhere on August 21, Tim finally got the call to fly to Phoenix where the Mets were playing. I was in shock, and relieved. Immediately, I made a one-way reservation to Phoenix as well. I was going to stay until Tim pitched. Unfortunately, it was a false alarm. The Mets were going to send Mike Jacobs down, but he hit four home runs in his first four days, and they decided to go with one less arm in the bullpen. Both Tim and I were in Phoenix for about 12 hours. Tim never left the hotel room. We were both devastated. Tim had waited 10 years for this moment. I had waited seven. I was immediately on the phone with Joe Kohm, and Marie, and they were offering me encouragement. Joe would always say, "Let's see what God is going to do." Later that night I had time to process how I felt and gather my thoughts.

FINALLY: A MAJOR LEAGUE REP

> *8/22/05*
>
> *Up at 4:30 am – smooth travel to Phoenix – surreal experience at first, but soon turned to uncertainty as no word came activating Tim – finally at 10 pm he was told to return to Norfolk – feelings of disbelief, anger, questioning God, etc – made a quick decision to fly home – avoided additional expense.*
>
> *Trusting God is difficult when these things happen. At least I got to see a Major League game. Up at 3:30 am (PST) – couldn't go back to sleep. Able to talk with Marie and Joe – a lot of venting; both were encouraging. Joe reminded me that I'm very close. He also reminded me that all God wants is for us to trust Him, even when there's no reason to. I need to be there for Tim.*

A story appeared in the *New York Post* the following Sunday. The headline read 'So close, yet so far.' It was about Tim. I had developed a relationship with Kevin Kernan, a sportswriter with the *New York Post*, and I told him what happened. He immediately said he would write about it, and he included me in the story. When the Assistant GM, Jim Duquette, found out I flew to Arizona as well, he told me he felt badly about it. Marie and I continued to pray for Tim to get called up and, when the rosters were expanded to 40 on September 1, Tim got the call again. This time it was for real. Tim was in the Majors, and Marie and I were praising God!

> *8/29/05*
>
> *Dear God: law practice is non-existent – I continue to need your guidance on what to do next. I have continued to see that, when I take initiative, things happen – that's been consistent.*

> *8/31/05*
>
> *Prayed for Tim to get called up – and it actually happened! What a stunning turn of events – but hard to get too excited with Hurricane disaster – the whole city of New Orleans is under water.*

I headed to New York at 5 am the day after Tim got the call. I arrived before 10 am, but I couldn't get in the stadium. I had bought some dress pants for Tim the night before, as Tim needed them for traveling with the team. The game wasn't until 1 pm, but once some of the front office staff arrived, I was able to hand over the pants. Tim didn't pitch that day, but he warmed up three times!

After the game, the Mets traveled to Florida to face the Marlins. That evening, I headed over to New Jersey to see Matt Hagen. He was playing independent ball for the New Jersey Jackals, and the home of Yogi Berra. I watched him play for an hour, but I was exhausted, and found the nearest hotel. I had seen a Major League game and an Independent league game in the same day, what a contrast in the level of play. But at least for one day, I was a Major League agent.

> *9/2/2005*
>
> *Home around lunchtime – greeted by Marie with a nice lunch and balloons. Re-connected and feeling supported. Worked for a few hours, and then the countdown to another game. Watched the game with Marie – lots of distractions with the kids, but finally they settled down. Thought that Tim wasn't coming in, but all of a sudden there he was*

on the pitcher's mound! Threw three fastballs to Carlos Delgado – 94 MPH – lined out – it was awesome! Earned himself another outing. It was an exciting moment.

The baseball season was extended for another month since the Major League regular season ends at the beginning of October. So I traveled to New York again, this time with Michael.

In the Mets Dugout with Tim – 9/17/2005

Michael in front of Shea Stadium – 9/17/2005

9/18/05

With God's help I made it through a long day – Tim didn't pitch again – so I'll wait another day. Otherwise, it was a day well spent with Michael – morning walk to restaurant; small Sunday school lesson; played together at the pool; and at the game by 11:15 – another field pass – watched batting practice – sat with Tim's girlfriend again – made some progress connecting with her; started to head home at 3:45 – home at 9:15 pm – that's a long day!

Michael had a great attitude – he watched the whole game on both days – I did say no a few times – overall it was a good bonding time – he will remember this weekend.

It felt like things had turned around. God was answering my prayers. My dreams were coming true. My family was supportive. It was all starting to feel worth it.

CHAPTER 16

The Offseason

> Preparation is everything.
> DAVID ROBINSON

As agents, Joe and I tried to do everything we could to help our players get to the Majors and stay there. It's hard enough to make it, but it's even harder to remain on that coveted 40-man roster. Therefore, we used the offseason as an opportunity to help our players get better.

Some organizations are better than others at player development, and most times it's done during "Instructs" after the season is over. Sometimes it happens in January, with a few of the organization's elite players. But for the rest of the players, they're pretty much on their own. With Tim, I took a vested interest, and I believe I played a role in him getting better.

After my first season with Tim, I arranged for him to work with Jimmy Mauder, a pitching coach who came highly recommended by some of my contacts. Even though Tim had four seasons of pro ball under his belt, he still was pretty raw when it came to pitching mechanics. Tim was a very quiet person, and some pitching coaches didn't take the time to communicate with him. The more outspoken players usually received the most instruction, as they would ask for the coach's opinion. Unfortunately, Tim kept to himself and didn't receive as much instruction as others.

Jimmy had several sessions with Tim. He worked on every aspect of Tim's delivery. I never realized there was so much to learn about throwing a baseball. From the windup, to the leg kick, to the delivery, Tim had a lot of moving parts. Some of it created deception, but the downside was inconsistency and lack of command. Jimmy helped Tim have a more consistent delivery.

Players also needed a good strength and conditioning program in the offseason. The teams give the players a basic offseason program, but there are plenty of strength and conditioning trainers who work with elite athletes. Each year I would try to hook up my players with some of the best trainers in the area. Some of the big agencies had their own training facilities, but these trainers could do just the same for them.

Two of the best trainers I knew were Kevin Maselka and Steve Horwitz. Kevin had worked with several professional basketball players, and he also helped Tim. Tim was already very strong and very big, but Kevin helped him work on his core, and not simply lift more weights. After a workout with Kevin, you would usually say it was the hardest workout you've ever done. Both Taylor and Aaron also worked out with Kevin when they were in Low A ball, and shared that sentiment.

Steve Horwitz is a chiropractor by trade, but also one of the best at strength and conditioning. Steve was the official chiropractor at the 1996 Olympics, so he has also worked with elite athletes. He had a unique ability to find the weakest link in a person's body. Steve would do an assessment with my players, and he would design a program that focused on my players' weaknesses. Without exception, the players focused on certain muscles they wouldn't have without Dr Horwitz's intervention.

My position players would benefit from hitting instruction from one of the best in the business, Mike Toomey, known as "Tooms." Mike Toomey is one of the best scouts I've ever known, and he loves to teach hitting. He taught two of my boys. Fortunately, Mike lived only ten minutes from my home, and he used a local hitting facility to teach all ages. I'd seen him teach a 50-year-old softball player and a ten-year-old just starting out, and everything in between. Mike had worked his way up to special assistant to the GM for the Kansas City Royals, and was on the road most of the time. However, there was a small window in January when Mike was available, and I arranged for several of my players to work with him. Even Taylor came down for a session, since he was pitching in the National League as a starter.

I usually footed the bill for the offseason training and instruction, so that wasn't helping the cash flow. But I saw it as an investment in my player's success, which meant success for me as well.

After Tim worked with Jimmy Mauder in the 1999 offseason, he also worked with several others as I continued to develop relationships with other pitching coaches. Mike Pazik, a former Major League pitcher, also lived in the area and worked with Mike Toomey at a local facility. Tim worked with him one offseason and, when Mike Pazik wasn't available the next year, I arranged for Tim to work with Steve Johnson, another former Major League pitcher who lived in the Baltimore area.

When Tim signed with the Mets as a free agent in the winter of 2004, I had him work with Craig Pippen, who happened to be good friends with Rick Peterson, the Mets' pitching coach at the time. Craig was a former minor league player, and big on using computers to analyze a player's pitching motion. He hooked up Tim and did an assessment, similar to what Dr.

Andrews did for many players in Atlanta. In fact, many teams sent their top players to Atlanta to get an analysis on the player's mechanics.

My partner, Joe, was a big believer in Tom House, a well-respected pitching coach in California with an unorthodox way of teaching. In the winter of 2004, I went with Joe and some of his players to San Diego to watch Tom work with players. It's always good to find an excuse to go to San Diego. Tom would spend three days with groups of pitchers, using a computer to analyze their motion and talk about his philosophy of pitching. I also used that opportunity to parlay an article in my law school newsletter, and their photographer was willing to take pictures of Joe and I for our brochure.

The offseason is also when the winter meetings take place every year in early December. The winter meetings started as a place where the minor league teams would get together and share ideas, and it blossomed into an incredible four days of deals and rumors of deals. Each Major League team has their entire front office staff in a suite, where they work 24/7 trying to make the next deal. Since every team is there, it's the ideal opportunity for teams to talk to each other. Of course, most agents are there as well, and they are also trying to make deals for their Major League free agents. Teams also looked to make deals with non-tendered players, and minor league free agents. It was usually the latter for me, but it was worthwhile to get some face time with the GMs, farm directors, and anyone else in the baseball industry.

The equipment companies are all there too, since there is a trade show going on at the same time. I tried to make appointments ahead of time with companies, like Nike and Reebok, who spend a lot of their time meeting with agents. But most of the time is spent hanging out in the lobby, and waiting for front office people to show their faces. Texting made it a lot easier to meet with people – *I'm in the lobby, when can we meet?*

Early in my career, I would try to hang out with people, who knew people, so I could get introduced. Whenever I hung out with Tooms, I got to meet everyone in the business. Tooms is the life of the party, and everyone wants to be around him. He tells a great story, and loves to share his adventures on the road. Someone I knew was able to get a job with an organization just by sitting around with Tooms, and meeting team representatives.

One year, Craig Pippen introduced me to Buddy Biancanala. Buddy played for the 1985 World Series Champions Kansas City Royals. He didn't have a great career, but he had a great world series and, as a result, he developed a mental approach to the game. He immediately wanted to help me with Aaron Laffey, as he noticed Aaron's walks were a bit high. That was a sign for him, as he believed walks were more of a mental lapse than anything else.

Buddy convinced me he could help Aaron, and Aaron soon became a disciple of Buddy's system. Buddy understands the athlete, and knows they perform best when they're in the zone. For Buddy, the zone is a place that doesn't just happen, but it can be created. For the pitcher, it can be created every pitch. He believes that, when your tense, your smaller muscles are not working, and that creates less fluidity. So basically, it's about relaxing and therefore allowing your muscle memory to do the work, requiring the brain to work less. Aaron believed in the system and, the following year, he had fewer walks.

Joe and I got excited about the weighted ball program used by Tom House. One of Joe's players, Steve Delabar, became the poster boy for the program. Due to an injury, Steve was out of baseball for three years. He was a teacher in Kentucky, and he began to use the weighted ball program. His velocity jumped from a high of 92 from three years prior, to a high of 98 after the program. He was referred to Joe, and had a job with the Mariners shortly thereafter. He made it to the Majors the same year.

We encouraged all our players to give the program a try, since most teams were going in the direction of pitchers with velocity of 95 MPH or greater. If done under the direction of someone who knows what they're doing, the program usually helped improve velocity by at least 2 to 3 MPH.

The offseason of 2005 was different, since the focus turned toward getting investors again. And while the offseason was typically a time for players to slow down, things in my life kept ramping up.

CHAPTER 17

Time for Investors

> **Plans fail for lack of counsel, but with
> many advisors they succeed.**
>
> PROV. 15:22

By the end of 2005, I finally had a player in the Majors, and at least three solid prospects in the stable. I made about $20,000 in the 2005 draft, and another $3,000 from Tim Hamulack for his month in the Majors[9].

My partner, Joe, also had a few prospects who had worked their way up the food chain, and were knocking on the Major League door. Even though we had formed an agency together, we each had our own players, with our own revenue and expenses. We envisioned merging everything at some point, but for the time being our focus was on encouraging each other and discussing any issues that came up.

---

[9] Since he signed as a minor league free agent the previous year, I still earned a percentage of his salary, even though he was making the Major League minimum.

My law practice had taken a big hit, as I didn't advertise and nor did I work to get new clients. Over the years, prior to the baseball business, I had built a pretty good client base. But many of my clients thought I was moving toward becoming a baseball agent, and with good reason. Revenue from my law practice went down each year. The conversations with Marie typically went the same way. She preferred that I work full-time in the law practice until I could earn enough income in baseball, but I felt I needed to invest more time on the baseball agency to get more players, and to keep my existing players. I just couldn't sit around and hope for things to work out.

By this time, and rightfully so, Marie had reached her limit on using our savings and the credit line. Something had to give. Ever since 2001, I had prepared a variety of plans to pitch to investors, and had given a presentation to a law firm a few years earlier when the *Post Magazine* article came out. The law firm rejected my proposal at the time but, by the end of 2005, I finally had some momentum. I put together another presentation, and was planning to give it to a family member and a friend.

But first, I wanted to make sure Marie was on board. We began meeting with another couple, and working through Marie's concerns.

11/20/05

We identified the problem with going forward with the business – Marie's not convinced it's God's will – so that needs to be resolved.

Around the end of 2005, Marie and I were under a lot of stress. In addition to our financial struggles, we were having various challenging issues with our boys.

Marie and I knew we needed help compromising and communicating, so we started going through a book called *Love & Respect*. The book helped us take a different look at how marriages can get on a crazy cycle that takes the relationship into reaction mode, and that perpetuates the cycle. The book, and its seminar, helped us learn new tools to stop our cycle. As our marriage got back on track, Marie was more open to me moving forward.

2/24/06

Long conversation with Marie – we talked for about four hours. Covered topics included: trips, camps, budget, investment plan – no argument – it was a breakthrough! Also talked about projects – lots of compromises – for the first time she referred to baseball as our commitment, not just my commitment. That brought tears to my eyes. It seems the Love & Respect series is having a positive effect on our marriage.

We pitched my plan to a family member and a couple of friends. They had faith in me, and were willing to give me $25,000/year for two years. In return, they wanted a piece of the action. The risk for them was minimal, as it was more like a no interest loan than an investment, but they would also get a small percentage of the revenue. I was thrilled; I had bought myself two more years.

Taylor Buchholz was on the forefront again as spring training began in 2006. He had been shut down again in August 2005, but I helped him find a doctor who did deep tissue massage, which helped him immensely with his shoulder. He was feeling good by the fall. He pitched very well in the prestigious Arizona fall league, which is a good indicator for success in the Majors.

The Houston Astros had a formidable rotation with Roger Clemens, Andy Pettitte, Roy Oswalt, and Brandon Backe. Taylor would be fighting for the 5th and final spot in the rotation. Meanwhile, Tim Hamulack was traded to the Dodgers in the offseason, in part because his minor league pitching coach, Dan Warthen, was now the bullpen coach for the Dodgers.

Ever since 1999, I had been traveling to Florida every spring training for four to five days, and attempted to see all my players. Up until 2006, I didn't have many players on teams with training facilities in Arizona, so I mainly went to Florida. For spring training in 2006, I had Tim Hamulack with the Dodgers in Vero Beach, Taylor Buchholz in Kissimmee with the Astros near Orlando, Aaron Laffey in Winter Haven with the Indians, and both Mike Costanzo and Marc Tugwell with the Phillies in Clearwater.

Just prior to leaving for Florida, Tim called to tell me he got optioned to the minors. Those phone calls are never pleasant, but it's also an opportunity to be there for my player. At least Tim was on the 40-man roster, so he would be considered when the need arose. I tried to keep it positive, telling him to stay focused. There are some things you can't control. The only thing you can control is throwing the ball.

However, upon arriving in Florida, I was greeted with a pleasant surprise. While having lunch with Taylor, Tim called to say he was back in the big leagues! The Dodgers decided to go with an extra pitcher. I figured Dan Warthen must have really fought for Tim. I could only describe it as a miracle, and certainly a hopeful sign for things to come.

3/29/06

Good 1st day – Straight to see Taylor – he was waiting for me – good conversation and I told him that I would pray for him. Then Tim H calls to tell me he's back in the big leagues – what a miracle!

Taylor was also having a great spring and, while I was still in Florida, Taylor pitched seven shutout innings in Atlanta in the Astros final spring training game, and he made the big league club as well! Taylor was the first rookie for the Astros to make the starting rotation out of spring training since John Halama in 1998. By the end of spring training, I had two players in the Majors.

I was excited, but it was also a time of unpredictability, not knowing how long they would stay in the Majors, and when I would see them pitch in person. I had been around long enough to know it was one thing to make it to the Majors, but the harder part was staying there. Most importantly, it meant I was going to be attending more Major League games – that was something new and exciting.

I was entering a new chapter in representing Major League players. I had developed relationships with other agents who represented players in the Majors, but I wasn't sure about what I could do for them. Possible marketing deals? Glove deals? Baseball card deals? I began feeling anxious about the future, and my ability to handle Major leaguers, but reminded myself God had a plan.

Taylor was scheduled to make his first start in San Francisco on April 11, so I got my airline ticket and headed west. As usual, things didn't work out as planned. From the moment I arrived in San Francisco, it rained, and rained, and rained some more. For the first time since 1961, the first two games of a Giant's home series were rained out. Finally, on the third day, a doubleheader was scheduled. Unfortunately, since the other starters now had enough rest, Taylor got bumped. I decided to attend the games anyway, since my flight didn't leave until the next morning.

But another unexpected event happened in the 2nd inning. The starter for the Astros, Brandon Backe, began to have pain in his elbow, and immediately Taylor began to warm up. Brandon came out, and Taylor went in.

Taylor pitched three innings, getting Barry Bonds out twice, one on a long fly ball to the warning track in centerfield. Taylor allowed a total of two runs on four hits, but for both Taylor and me, the outing was six years of hard work, and a moment we would always remember. I got in touch with Bobby Evans, the Giants farm director, and he helped me make it down to the locker room doors in between games. I asked Taylor to sign and date a baseball. It was a God moment.

4/14/2006

Read the Bible this morning. While in prayer, I was reminded that today is Good Friday. Reflected on what Jesus did for me. I pray I will continue to be faithful to share God's word with those who come across my path.

Taylor faces Barry Bonds on April 13, 2006 in San Francisco

Tim Hamulack started off well for the Dodgers. Through the month of April, he had a respectable 1.69 ERA in twelve outings. However, the month of May wasn't as kind to Tim, and his ERA jumped to 5.73. After two outings against Philly, in the beginning of June where he allowed two runs in each outing, he was optioned to AAA. He wouldn't come back again until the end of August, where he finished the season with a 6.34 ERA. Although I had no idea at the time, Tim would never make it back to the Majors.

Taylor followed up his first outing with four quality starts in a row, including a two-hit shutout in 8 ⅔ innings against the Pirates. He didn't fare too well in three of the next four outings, allowing at least eight runs in the three bad outings, mixed in with a nine-inning shutout against the Rangers.

Taylor managed to stay in the Majors until he was optioned on July 27. That was Taylor's last option. We found out the next year that it turned out to be the best thing to happen for him. He was called back up in September, and that was significant because it gave him a total of 140 days in the Majors, and kept open the possibility of being eligible for arbitration in just two more years.

As all this unfolded, I managed to take Michael and Jonny on two separate trips. Sammy was still too young. First, I took Michael to Texas to see Taylor pitch in a AAA game. We flew into Houston and drove a couple hours to Round Rock, where Houston's AAA affiliate was at the time. It was an adventure. We watched Taylor pitch, and we met up with him and his new girlfriend, Ashley (his future wife), after the game for dinner. I looked up some old friends in Austin, and they invited us to stay with them. When we traveled back to Houston, Michael asked if we could go to an Astro's game. I wisely said yes. I can still remember the smile on his face as we walked to the stadium.

With Michael in Round Round TX August 2006

The following week, it was Jon's turn. We headed down to Tampa to see Mike Costanzo play at Clearwater, the Phillies' Hi A team. Costanzo had skipped low A and was sent to Hi-A for the 2006 season. Mike had his usual slow start, but he picked it up again. Jon was, and still is, an avid skateboarder, so Florida was a good match for him since it offered some of the best skateparks in the country. The Tampa skatepark was almost Heaven for Jonny. He had never seen so many ramps. He could handle most of them, except for the big 30-foot ramp outside. We bounced back and forth from the Tampa skatepark to the Clearwater 688. We also saw Mike play three games in 100 degrees heat, and attended a small church on Sunday. Whenever and wherever I was on a Sunday, I almost always found a church to attend.

I was somewhat relieved once the 2006 season was over. The daily pressures for the players to perform had taken its toll on them, and on me. I was ready to focus on my law practice, and I was okay with working on cases, provided the work wasn't too stressful. I had taken on another jury trial, and that had caused stress during August, but it was over in one day and I moved on, vowing once again to not take on any more jury trials! During 2006, my law practice picked up, so I decided to forgo getting another $50,000 from investors.

During the 2006 offseason, Taylor was traded again. I remember being in Florida for the winter meetings, and there were rumors on the last day that Taylor was going to be traded to the White Sox, but that fell through. About a week later, he was traded to the Colorado Rockies in the Jason Jennings trade. The Rockies projected Taylor more as a reliever, and Taylor was okay with going to the bullpen. It certainly did not bring in nearly as much money as starting pitchers but, with Taylor being out of options, he was told early in spring training in 2007 that he had made the club as a reliever.

Wrigley Field, June 25, 2007 to see Taylor and visit friends and relatives

Taylor managed to stay in the Majors during the entire 2007 season. He finished with a respectable 4.23 ERA, and started in six games early in the season. The 2007 season was also the year the Rockies went to the World Series. Taylor pitched 1.2 innings in relief, in the one-game playoff win against the Padres.

The 2007 season also marked another Major League debut. Aaron Laffey was quietly making his way through the Indian's minor league system, starting out the 2007 season in AA, and quickly getting promoted to AAA where he compiled a 3.08 ERA in 15 starts. As momentum built, I took a quick flight to Buffalo in July to see his start. His whole family was there, and he had another quality start. (At least six innings pitched allowing three runs or less.) At dinner afterwards, I shared some scripture about surrendering to God, and told Aaron the next time I would see him, it would be in Cleveland.

Aaron was called up to the Majors the next week, to start against the Minnesota Twins on August 4, 2007. Just a few days earlier, one of the main bridges in Minneapolis collapsed, and we weren't certain if they would cancel the game. I flew to Minneapolis and, of course, it was raining. At least this time there wouldn't be a rainout, as they played under a dome! Aaron had a good debut. He went 5.1 innings, allowing three runs. His whole family was there. For the third time, I was able to hear another one of my players announced over the loudspeakers. Whenever I heard their names, it reminded me of the *Washington Post* article from 2002:

> *Pasti is convinced that he'll someday hear the name of his player…*

I was right!

Aaron had made it to the Majors at 22 years of age. He had moved through the minor league system in four years, which is impressive for a high school draft pick. It's not unusual for high school players to take five to seven years to get to the Majors. The Indians' GM, Mark Shapiro, always liked Aaron. He also thought Aaron had a lot of moxie. Aaron certainly showed his moxie on his minor league debut during 2003 in Princeton, West Virginia. I will always remember Aaron calling off the catcher on a few occasions. Many pitchers shake off their catchers but rarely does an 18-year-old rookie do it! It was unforgettable.

Aaron Laffey MLB debut – August 4, 2007

Aaron was sent down after the game, and came back up at the end of August. The Indians were also in the playoffs, and went up three games to one against the Red Sox. It was looking like a Rockies versus Indians World Series, as the Rockies were taking care of business in the National League. Could I have two players in the World Series? What were the chances of that since I only had two players in the Majors, and they played on teams that rarely made it to the playoffs!? It was a fun thought.

Aaron was on the playoff roster, and pitched 4.1 innings of scoreless relief in game five in Fenway Park, which saved their bullpen. But it wasn't meant to be for the Indians. They lost the next three games, and were sent packing their bags. Aaron would only pitch in that one game, but his outing was another feather in his cap and, once again, showed his moxie.

Taylor did not pitch in the playoff series against the Phillies and the Diamondbacks and, with Aaron Cook coming off the DL, the Rockies decided to take Taylor off the active roster for the World Series. I went from having two players in the World Series to zero. Taylor would still suit up, and I would still get a picture with him at Coors Field, but that was the only highlight for me. Taylor still received a nice playoff share, so he was happy. And he had another full year in the Majors, so I was happy.

At Coors Field, World Series - October 2007

At the end of 2007, I went out to dinner with Marie, and we talked about the future. Fortunately, it was a good conversation. But I was anxious about the upcoming year.

12/30/07

Out to dinner with Marie – good conversation prior to dinner about things on her heart, and I shared about my anxieties with the upcoming year – told her I was tired of not making money – something needs to happen – if Taylor gets hurt, I don't know what I'm going to do – open to God – Marie was encouraged, feeling that I'm open to God's leading.

CHAPTER 18

Fish or Cut Bait

*Instead you ought to say, If the Lord wills,
we will live and also do this or that.*

JAMES 4:15

The 2008 season brought another fish-or-cut-bait moment. After much prayer and discussions with Marie, we decided if Taylor didn't make it to arbitration by the end of the 2008 season, I would take that as a sign God was closing the doors on the baseball agency. Once a player makes it to arbitration, he can make significantly more money. Prior to arbitration, the players make just a little over the Major League minimum, and therefore the agent fee is minimal. But if he was eligible, I would continue on the same path. Some would call that a fleece, seeking God's will through a predetermined sign, but it was also a reality. At some point, I had to earn some money or move on. We had finally reached that point again.

I figured that if Taylor was in the Majors for the entire year, he would finish with 2.140 in service time, or two years and 140 days. To be eligible for arbitration, a player had to have three years of service time, or be in the top 17% of players with less than three years, and more than two years of service time (also known as a Super Two). Basically, you take all the players with more than two years, and less than three years of service, and multiply the total number by 17%. Looking back on the previous ten years, 2.140 was always enough to get in the top 17%.

On the recruiting front, I had secured a left-handed hitting catcher at Coastal Carolina, named Charles "Dock" Doyle. Ever since representing Mike Costanzo in the 2005 draft, I got in the door with other prospects there. Coastal Carolina was becoming a strong baseball program and, with the location near Myrtle Beach and the warmer weather, the coach was able to get some good prospects from the Northeast.

I headed down to Charlottesville to see Dock play against the University of Virginia. It was certainly closer than going to Myrtle Beach, and I knew there would be a lot of scouts in attendance to see the UVA players. As I do at every game, I was also on the lookout for other prospects, and I noticed another player pitch, and immediately could tell he was a prospect. His name was Pete Andrelczyk, a teammate of Dock's.

One of the scouts in attendance was Mike Elias, with the Cardinals[10]. I struck up a conversation with him, and he confirmed Pete's prospect status. I quickly met up with Pete, and he agreed to hire me as his advisor.

I continued my tradition of traveling to spring training. I headed to both Arizona and Florida, as I had prospects in both places. I always made sure to talk with front office staff to get some face time, and a sense of where my players stood in their eyes. On my last day in Florida, I took a

---

[10] Mike Elias is now the General Manager for the Baltimore Orioles.

walk on the beach and wrote postcards to my wife, kids, and to myself. I kept the postcard I wrote to myself:

> *You have come a long way in just one year. All of your players are making progress – even Tim, who was out all last year. There is finally a light at the end of the tunnel. Yes, this is about pursuing your passion, but it's God who gave you this passion. Continue to trust Him to lead you. Make sure that you take care of your family along the way. Continue to view the law cases as a positive thing. You may still want to take cases, even when you don't need to. 3/13/08*

As the season began, Taylor had a secure spot in the Rockies' bullpen. Aaron competed for a spot in the rotation, but lost out to Cliff Lee for the final spot. Aaron had replaced Cliff in his 2007 debut, when Cliff was demoted to AAA – hard to believe, but true. Tim Hamulack had signed with the Royals in the off-season after undergoing season-ending Tommy John surgery, and missing most of 2007. He was invited to Major League camp, but sent to AAA to start the season. Mike Costanzo was traded twice during the off-season, first to the Astros, and then to the Orioles a week later. He had a good spring training at Major League camp, but he started the season at AAA in Norfolk, Virginia.

I made it a point to see all my players, whether they were prospects or not. The remainder of my stable included: Jon Link, who was putting together a few good seasons with the White Sox organization; Mike Penn, an 11th round pick by the Royals who was referred to me by Tom Rust, a Christian involved in discipleship ministry whom I met at spring training a few years earlier; Dan McDonald, an 8th round pick by the Mets in the 2007 draft, whom I met at Cape Cod and was his advisor; Derek McDaid, a non-draft free agent with the Padres who I helped get a job from independent ball to affiliated ball; and Bryan Pritz and Ben Zeskind, both signed out of the University of Richmond. Ben was a late round pick by the Blue Jays, and Bryan was a non-draft free agent signing by the Red Sox. After making my rounds throughout Arizona and Florida, I was ready for the season.

As the 2008 baseball season started, I took the opportunity to see Mike Costanzo in Norfolk on take-your-child-to-work day. It was an all-day road trip, with all three of my boys – Jon, Michael, and Sammy. It was an easy decision for Marie to stay home, as I had recently been on many road trips without any of the boys. This also gave me an opportunity to hook up with Joe Kohm, as he resided in Virginia Beach. It was a beautiful spring day. Although the traffic was horrendous, I didn't mind as I laughed with my boys in the car, and appreciated seeing my partner and one of my players.

Take your child to work day, Norfolk VA 4/24/2008

Soon thereafter, I received a call from Mike Sheridan's father, who resided in Washington, DC. Mike was a junior at William & Mary and was batting over .400. It was a rare thing to be on the receiving end of a phone call from a prospect. Usually the players, who initiated calling me, were not prospects and thought I could get them noticed. I would tell them that unless they were getting looked at by scouts, I couldn't help. But after talking with a few scouts, I believed Mike needed an advisor, and I immediately met with his parents at their home. The coach at William & Mary had asked around about me, and Mr. Sheridan said I checked out: *A Christian man, upright and honest.* That was an encouragement and, more importantly, they got back to me within a week and asked me to be Mike's advisor.

It was going to be a busy spring, as I had a total of four players in the draft: Dock Doyle and Pete Andrelczyk from Coastal Carolina; Mike Sheridan from William & Mary; and Ryan Wood from East Carolina, whom I had advised out of high school, and was now a junior and eligible for the draft.

On top of that, Marie had agreed to get a dog, and we were going through the process of finding the right one for our family. Although she was not a dog person, she was outnumbered, with all the boys and me urging her. Of course, the boys said they would help. And we hoped a dog would calm things down a bit by having something for the boys to focus on. I agreed to let Marie pick out the dog, and we settled on a laid-back Beagle. But when I went on road trips, Marie ended up caring for three boys and a dog! Things were not getting much better for her, but I was in the fast lane with lots of plates in the air, and didn't feel like I could slow down.

It didn't take long before Aaron Laffey was back in the Majors. In his first start at the end of April, he had a no hitter through five innings against the Yankees. But after a few tough breaks, and a broken bat single, four runs came in. Still, it was good enough for him to stay in the Majors for another start. In the meantime, Taylor was slowly working his way to the back of the bullpen, coming in later in games, and even earning his first career save.

May 2008 was probably the busiest month I can remember. Not only was it Mother's Day, my birthday, my wife's birthday, and our anniversary, but I had two players in the Majors and four players in the draft. I had been traveling a lot the previous years, but spring of 2008 took it to a new level.

Still, it was a very exciting month. Aaron was named AL Rookie of the Month, with five outings and a 2.08 ERA. I saw him pitch seven innings in Cleveland on my birthday. It was an afternoon game, so I drove six hours in the morning, and then six hours back home after the game. It was a good way to celebrate my birthday, especially since Aaron allowed only one run, and got the win!

After returning home, I was back on the road to Norfolk, William & Mary, East Carolina, and Myrtle Beach, all in three days. I saw Mike Costanzo play again. Mike was beginning to improve after his usual slow start. He had done so well at spring training, and now he was pressing to get to the Majors. It wasn't working.

Then I traveled to William & Mary, about a 45-minute drive from Norfolk. I watched another game, and finally met up with Mike Sheridan around 11 pm. I had already got a blessing from his parents, but I needed to meet Mike to confirm he wanted me to advise him. He did.

The next morning, I was back on the road to East Carolina to see Ryan Wood. There were some cross-checkers there, but they weren't there to see Ryan. Still, they all said Ryan was a projectable player and, at 6ft 4 and 200 lbs, it was easy to see why. Unfortunately, Ryan never did fill out and, due to injuries, he never reached his potential. I started to feel a little bit like a scout as I made my way down to Myrtle Beach, as scouts are on the road throughout spring. At the very least, it felt good that I was taking the time to see the players in person. It would pay off in giving them good advice.

It was a smooth trip down to Myrtle Beach, and I had a little downtime to "comb" the beach, as my father would always say. The beach was always a place where I felt most at peace. Maybe it was the peace I felt at Lake Michigan as a child, or maybe I could always count on the beach to be the same. Either way, I knew it was good for my soul, and therefore it was always a priority.

At the game, there were some scouts "sitting on" Pete Andrelczyk to see him pitch. It was always hard for scouts to see relievers and, sometimes, they would have to watch all three games of a series before they got a glimpse. But that helped Dock Doyle, as many scouts saw him play all three games and, since he played well, he earned some money that weekend by moving up the draft board.

After watching two of the three games, I started to head home on Saturday evening. I figured I could get most of the way, and then get up early to be home in time for Mother's Day breakfast, a tradition in the Pasti home. I had talked to the older boys, and they got started on breakfast. I made it home in time. It wasn't the best day for my wife, as the dog threw up on her mother's shoe (with her feet in the shoes!) and we watched Sammy play a baseball game in the rain, and lose 23 to 2. But at least I was home for Mother's Day. It was the effort that counts.

For the rest of the month, I made trips to Wilmington, North Carolina for the CAA tournament, to Danville, Virginia for the Big South tournament, and to Philadelphia with my son Michael to see Taylor. Also, Marie and I managed a quick trip away to celebrate our 16th wedding anniversary.

The travel during May paid off, as Mike Sheridan, Pete Andrelczyk, and Dock Doyle were all drafted in the 5th round. All three of them continued to move up the draft board, as they were playing well and considered to be signable players. I was convinced that, if they did not have an advisor, they would not have known how to respond to the scouts, and they would not have been drafted as high. They all received slot money, and I earned over $16,000 in the draft. The money felt like a bonus, since I had none of these players at the beginning of the year.

Still, there was more to come. One of the highlights of the year was in June, when Cleveland played in Colorado. It was a rare matchup for inter-league play, the two teams rarely face one another. It would also be the first and last time I had a player on opposing teams play in the same game. It was a no brainer for me to fly to Colorado to see both Aaron and Taylor. When Taylor and Aaron were early in their careers, I invited them to get a workout from Kevin Maselka, so they had previously met. We all grabbed lunch together in Colorado. Also, I had previously developed a relationship with the Rockies community operations guy, and he arranged for me to get a picture of both Aaron and Taylor before the game on the field. If you come to my office today, you will see that picture on the wall.

6/18/08

Connected with Jason Patterson of Timeless Sports – lots of possibilities there. Then, the game – Laffey 6 ip – 3 runs – got behind too much. Still, kept them in the game – Taylor came in 8th inning and did his thing. Rockies won 4-2. Taylor could make the all-stars.

With Aaron and Taylor, Coors Field – 6/17/2008

During this busy period, Marie had been a trooper. Similar to being a baseball wife, also known as a baseball widow, pursuing my dream had put a lot on her, especially with three boys. But, as we headed to Wisconsin for a family trip to celebrate her parent's 50th wedding anniversary in her father's hometown of Janesville, Wisconsin, we had another breakthrough.

We had been studying the DISC personality assessment[11] and found a couple in Indiana that offered DISC workshops for couples. I contacted them and, although they didn't have any upcoming workshops, they agreed to meet with us on our way to Wisconsin.

---

[11] DISC stands for Dominant (get it done person); Influential (get excited); Conscientious (get it right); and Steady (get along).

> *6/27/08*
>
> *What a tremendous blessing it was to meet with the Spasics. Right from the start they were just what we needed. Good time at lunch at Applebees – kids did great; then to their church for a 1½ hour meeting. Marie said she felt like we were in the presence of God – another light bulb went off, as I saw hope as to how we can move forward. We need to yield more to each other; communicate our needs; use each other's strengths.*

As it turned out, Taylor stayed in the Majors for the entire 2008 season. Not only that, he was also one of the best setup guys in the Major Leagues. He finished the season with a 2.17 ERA as an 8th inning setup guy for the Rockies. When I attended the annual agent meeting in New York City, the Player's association calculated the pool of players, and Taylor was the last guy eligible for arbitration! I felt like I belonged. It was certainly a sign for me to continue moving forward. The best part, Marie agreed.

We finished out the year with a family trip to the Reebok store to use $500 in merchandise from Mike Costanzo, as I had also negotiated a deal for him with the brand at the winter meetings. Things were looking up, and I felt rejuvenated.

CHAPTER 19

Arbitration

> Whatever you do, whether in word or deed, do it in the name of the Lord Jesus Christ, giving thanks to God the Father through Him.
>
> COL. 3:17

An agent doesn't earn much compensation during the player's first few years in the Majors. The teams don't pay the players much more than the Major League minimum, which had risen to $400,000, and the agents can't earn a fee that would take the player's salary under the minimum. So if a player makes $410,000, the agent could earn no more than $10,000, the amount the player made over the minimum. But it's also difficult to take the entire amount over the minimum. Since the larger agencies don't charge a fee until a player makes it to arbitration, there's always a risk of losing a player by asking for a fee during those pre-arbitration years.

Either way, I hadn't made much in agent fees up until this point, except money received from signing bonuses in the draft, some agent fees, and a few baseball card deals for some of my players who were considered prospects. Realistically, time had almost run out. However, since Taylor was eligible for arbitration, I was looking at $40,000 in fees. I could supplement that amount with my law practice, and that would be enough to keep me going.

The arbitration process is where an agent earns his wings. Having Taylor eligible for arbitration was also an opportunity to use my skills as a lawyer. I had been attending the agents' meetings every year since 2003, so I knew the basics. Each year, the Player's association spends most of the daylong meeting on educating the agents on the ins and outs of the arbitration process. The teams have an advantage with the support they receive from the commissioners' office.

A year prior, I had taken a quick two-day trip to Florida, where the arbitration hearings were held that February. Certified agents are allowed to sit in on the hearing, so that helped me begin my preparation in anticipation of Taylor being eligible at the end of the season.

The first year I had an eligible player was also the first year the Player's association implemented a new requirement for agents. They wanted each agent to submit who was assisting the agent in preparing for arbitration. They were especially concerned about agents who had never done an arbitration case. They knew a bad deal would adversely affect other cases. It's like selling a house below market value. If they felt you were not experienced enough, they would force you to align with a more experienced agent.

More importantly, the teams target inexperienced agents by trying to make a pre-tender deal. Basically, even if a player is eligible for arbitration, a team could decide the player isn't worth the amount of money he could earn through the process, and decide to non-tender him. The player then becomes a free agent, and can sign with any team, but that is usually not the preferred way to go. As a negotiation tactic, teams would tell the agent they were considering non-tendering a player, to convince the agent a pre-tender would be better. Of course, that is not true. The salary figures each year support the conclusion that the deeper you go in the process, the better the deal.

The arbitration process starts on the tender date, which is usually around December 12. If a team tenders an arbitration eligible player, that player is going to sign a Major League contract for the following year. The amount of that contract will be negotiated by comparing previous year's contracts for similar players, with similar service time. If a player is non-tendered, that player is a free agent, and can sign with any team. With a few exceptions, players will get more when they're tendered.

Once a player is tendered, the next important date is the exchange of numbers date, usually the day after Martin Luther King Day in January. On that day, the team and the player submit a salary number. If the case goes to a hearing, the arbitration panel can only choose one of those numbers. Once those two numbers are submitted, it creates a midpoint. The midpoint is the number you to get over for the arbitration panel rule in your favor.

For example, if a player submits $1,200,000, and the team submits $900,000, the midpoint is $1,050,000. If the arbitration panel believes your player is worth a penny above $1,050,000, you win and will receive $1,200,000 for the next season. The hard part is you don't know what number the other team is going to submit, so most cases settle just before the exchange of numbers.

As I began to prepare for arbitration, I knew we had some leverage since the most important year of a player's career, in his first year of arbitration, is his most recent year. It's called his platform year. Taylor had a great platform year. But the downside was he didn't have a lot of bulk meaning, as a Super Two, he had a lot less innings pitched than his comparables.

More importantly, Taylor had been a starter in his first season, and a middle reliever in his second season, so he couldn't compare to those set-up guys who had three years in that role. Unfortunately, when a pitcher changes his role, he will be compared with others who have a similar role. In other words, he wouldn't get much credit for his starts since he was no longer a starter. If he had some starts in his platform year (his most recent year), we could argue he still had a role as a spot starter.

When the Rockies contacted me early in the process, I knew Taylor would get tendered, so I told them to get back to me after the tender date. Soon thereafter, the Rockies called again to begin the negotiation process. The mantra from the player's association is to arbitrate before you negotiate. It was a good mantra. It's always better to know the player's value, and have a target number before you enter any negotiation. I had prepared early in the process, and felt comfortable with the value I put on Taylor.

The Rockies strategy focused on comparables from the 2005 season, which was an older market with lower salaries. They had a pretty good comparable in Dan Wheeler, who also had a great platform season as a set-up guy, and very little bulk. Certainly, I knew a most recent comparable is the best comparable. However, I had also noticed another player from the 2005 season, Brendan Donnelly, was helpful because he had a lot of bulk and yet he signed for the same amount as Dan Wheeler.

As I looked closer at Wheeler and Donnelly, I compared the number of "holds," a more recent statistic given to relievers who hold the lead for the starting pitcher, but don't get a save because they don't pitch in the 9th inning. Although Donnelly had a significant number of holds compared to Wheeler, Donnelly's holds were primarily in the 7th inning, and Wheeler's holds were in the 8th inning. Since both Donnelly and Wheeler signed for the same amount, I figured I could argue that Taylor should get close to Scott Proctor, who had a lot of bulk and was part of the pool from the most recent arbitration season. Proctor also had mostly 7th inning holds and Taylor had mostly 8th inning holds.

When the player's association contacted me to check in, I shared my findings. To my surprise, they were not pleased with my comparison. They didn't want me to use comparables from three years ago. I tried to explain my reasoning, but the more I tried to explain, the more concerned they got. It got to the point where the player's association wanted to see all my exhibits. I was in danger of the player's association contacting my player, and recommending I get assistance.

As I put my exhibits together, I had assistance from Joe, and a former intern who had a knack for putting the statistics in easy-to-read charts. I was also able to use charts to explain my argument. I submitted 38 exhibits, and finally the player's association let me continue handling the case myself. My legal experience paid off.

The Rockies' first offer was $950,000, based in part on Wheeler's salary from three years earlier. I argued that Taylor was more in line with Scott Proctor's salary ($1.1 million), and I asked them to give me a comparable from the previous year. They were always reluctant to give me a name. I pointed out that the comparables who signed for $950,000 the previous year, were players who were primarily used in the 7th inning.

The player's association had Taylor at $1 million plus. I valued Taylor higher. In their minds, anything over $1 million was acceptable. I continued to stay with my figure of $1.1 million as we approached the exchange of numbers date. The Rockies thought I was just negotiating, but I really believed Taylor was worth that much. But there was still room to compromise. In fact, the process was designed to bring the parties toward a settlement, rather than risk an either-or solution.

The night before the exchange of numbers, the Rockies made their final offer of $1,055,000. We turned it down.

ARBITRATION

> *1/19/09 (Martin Luther King Day)*
>
> *Waited all day before I finally got a call from the Rockies at 5 pm – things moved quickly – they offered $1,040,000, then $1,050,000 – then waited until 10:30 pm for them to come up to $1,055,000. Didn't accept – we were at $1,067,000.*

The next morning I spoke with Taylor, and he was more inclined to try to reach a settlement. He reasoned that it wasn't worth $12,000 to go through arbitration, and face the possibility of getting less. We could still exchange numbers and settle, but I told him I would call the Rockies one more time. In the meantime, we had to give our number to the player's association, just in case. Our figure was $1.2 million. We just needed to create a midpoint. I figured they would come in at no more than $950,000, creating a midpoint of $1,075,000.

In our last conversation, the Rockies offered another $40,000 in incentives if Taylor finished a certain number of games. That was enough to close the deal, and we had a number that met the players association approval. It was a good negotiation, and Taylor was pleased with how it turned out. He ended up being the first non-closing super two relief pitcher to get over $1 million. Unfortunately, I didn't have any time to celebrate since I had taken on a serious criminal case, and it was looking more like a jury trial even though I said I would never take another jury trial! But I did what was needed to support the family.

Both Marie and I had been in survival mode for six months before the settlement, and then for another couple months as I worked on the four-day jury trial in February. No other time in our marriage were we so busy. But this would turn out to be my final jury trial.

CHAPTER 20

Letting Go

> If any man wishes to come after me, he must deny
> himself, and take up his cross and follow me.
>
> MATT. 16:24

The excitement of Taylor's signing was short-lived, as Taylor was shut down in 2009 during spring training with pain in his elbow. The Rockies initially recommended rehab but, when Taylor continued to have pain, an MRI revealed a torn ligament requiring Tommy John surgery. Taylor would be out for the season. The only good news was that Taylor still received his salary for the season, and I received my agent fees.

Then, at the end of the 2009 season, the Rockies agreed to tender Taylor again, even though Taylor didn't throw one pitch all season. They were counting on the success rate of Tommy John surgery, and they figured a $1.055 million dollar investment was worth it. There were comparables where players sat out all season and received the same salary, so the Rockies gave in, and I was going to earn another $42,000 for the 2010 season.

During this time, I came across an interesting book called the *Dream Giver* by Bruce Wilkinson. The author understood dreams and, although he would agree there is no formula for success, he believed there were several identifiable stages to every dream.

According to Wilkinson, the story of Exodus reveals a pattern that is repeated throughout the Bible whenever God's people reach for their dream, and attempt great things for Him. In almost every instance, they:

1. Become aware of a personal dream or calling, then decide to pursue it.
2. Face fear as they leave a place of comfort.
3. Encounter opposition from those around them.
4. Endure a season of difficulty that tests their faith – the desert.
5. Learn the importance of surrender and consecration to God – letting go of the dream.
6. Fight the giants that stand between them and the fulfillment of their dream.
7. Reach their full potential as they achieve their dream and bring honor to God.

As I continued to explore the stages, I was amazed at how many stages I had been through. Clearly, I had been through the desert stage, and had met the giants that prevented me from going forward.

But there was an interesting stage I had never thought about – letting go and surrendering the dream to God. After all, if God puts the desires in our hearts, our dreams are really His to begin with. Moreover, Wilkinson knew that if we don't let go of our dreams, they can become our source of happiness. We can be so attached to our dreams, we become miserable if we don't achieve them. I began to realize that surrendering the dream would allow God to re-shape my desires to His purposes. I also came to the realization that I was too attached to this dream of being a baseball agent. I had somehow gotten it into my mind that, if I didn't achieve this dream, I would end up like my father – filled with regret at the end of my life. I was living in fear, and this was driving my ambition.

I decided it was time to let go. I could still pursue my goals, but I didn't have to be attached to them. As I began to mentally let go, I could feel the weight lifted off my shoulders. I shifted my focus to searching out what God wanted me to do with my life, not simply concluding that I was doing God's will. I asked God for wisdom and, for the first time, felt like I was fully surrendered. I had initially surrendered when I first became a Christian, but there were areas of my life I was still holding on to. I feared that if I completely surrendered to God, He would send me to China as a missionary. But I was learning that's not how He works. He knows our hearts and dreams. I started trusting Him with mine. I turned to my journal a lot to process where God was leading.

2/14/10

Told Marie my continuing struggles – God seems to be silent on what direction I should go – How long do I persevere? I feel I'm willing to do what God wants me to do.

2/22/10

Quiet time – I'm beginning to see that I'm unable to see God's will, as I'm more focused on what God will do for me, not what I can do for God. God wants to use my gifts for his purpose.

> *2/25/10*
>
> *Finally back to God's word in the morning – hoping to get perspective for the day. I am willing to submit to God's will – and I continue to pray for direction – Estate Planning seems appealing – but that will take time to develop – trial work just causes me too much stress.*

> *4/23/10*
>
> *My law practice is picking up – and I see more purpose in what I'm doing.*

The 2010 draft came and went without any prospects. I was unable to build on my successes from previous drafts and, having Major League players, didn't seem to make a difference. I was in the running for a high school prospect who was a potential 1st round pick, but a scout directed the player to an agent who was more likely to convince him to sign rather than go to college.

Taylor started his rehab assignment in May 2010, but I got a call from the GM of the Rockies who told me Taylor wasn't going to pitch for a while because he was diagnosed with depression and anxiety. I was in shock. I couldn't believe what I heard. I didn't see it coming, and neither did Taylor's wife who was equally surprised to hear the news. Fortunately, I understood what Taylor was going through. I had a family member experience this, and I knew it could happen to anyone. In most cases, it's treatable with therapy, and the right medication. But in the world of a professional athlete, where the player is under a microscope, it is much harder to return to the public eye.

6/5/10

To Tilghman island – went for a walk with Marie – told her where I'm at with work – it's ongoing – but she suggested that I consider being more open to what God would have me do, including giving up baseball – I'm willing if that is what God wants me to do.

6/14/10

Yes, I am sad that baseball may not work out – but I also believe that I'm facing it – my biggest fear is having to work for someone else.

6/16/10

I'm coming to the end of my belief that this is what I'm supposed to do – at some point God should show me what these setbacks must mean or that I should do something else.

At Tilghman Island with Marie - 6/5/2010

Thankfully, Taylor got to the point where he was activated and back in the Majors in a few months. Since the Rockies were fighting for a playoff spot, they didn't give him much of an opportunity to show he could succeed. They placed him on the disabled list in August, and finally designated him for assignment. He was claimed by the Blue Jays, but they didn't have any information about Taylor's condition.

I talked with the Rockies' GM, and questioned him for designating Taylor rather than putting him back on the disabled list. When a team designates a player, he goes through waivers, and is either picked up by another team, elects free agency, or agrees to go to AAA. I felt they were kicking Taylor while he was down. The GM didn't like my questions, and went on the attack. He told me everyone in the front office says I don't trust them, and they don't like dealing with me. Since I'd never had a problem with anyone there, I figured that was his way of dealing with conflict and I let it go.

The Blue Jays claimed Taylor, but he only pitched in two games during the last two weeks of September. They heard through the grapevine about his mental health, and decided to not take any chances. After the season ended, Taylor was designated again by the Blue Jays, and claimed by the Red Sox. After the Red Sox learned of Taylor's past, they non-tendered him, and Taylor became a free agent.

Meanwhile, I moved back to the office where I had started my law practice back in 1992. A few of the same lawyers were still there, and I could get extra work from them. Ironically, I was doing what my wife had always suggested. She noticed the changes in me, as I told her I needed emotional support and wanted to hear how she felt. As I prayed for God to help me make good choices, I told Marie that I would do what she wanted. She asked me what changed. I was including her more in my decisions. I said I wanted her support, and I wanted her to feel heard. We were making progress.

I was working full-time as a lawyer again. I felt a new appreciation for the practice of law. I was even able to handle family law cases, an area I had never previously wanted to do. I was still able to be a baseball agent, but that wasn't driving my schedule or income anymore.

Even though I had let go of the dream, I still had a handful of clients, and Joe and I still helped with each other's players. I wasn't ready to give up going to Florida every year for spring training, and I would continue to attend games when my players were within driving distance. But as I let go, I felt a new sense of peace, and a definite shift in my relationship with God. I approached each day differently. I began looking for opportunities to serve God in tangible ways. Our church had been going to Fairmont, West Virginia, each year to work on homes and host a Vacation Bible School at a local church. I had taken the two older boys back in 2005 and, in 2011, it was time to take the whole family.

7/21/11

God used me in a powerful way. This trip has been about reaching out to the community. I have seen God work through me. I have seen things occur that could have only happened by God's divine intervention. I need to continue to put myself in situations where it's beyond my own ability to have success.

CHAPTER 21

Not All It's Cracked Up To Be

> You may think the grass is greener on the other side. But if you take the time to water your own grass it would be just as green.
>
> HENRY FORD

When I would tell people I was a baseball agent, they usually say something like, "That must be a cool job." Their perception typically came from the movie *Jerry Maguire*, and they pictured me traveling all over the country going to baseball games. Sure, there were moments when I sat in the stands of a Major League game, and watched one of my players realize their dream. I was fortunate to be a part of that process for four different players.

Unfortunately, there are many aspects of being a sports' agent most people don't understand. First and foremost, there is an intense pressure for the player to succeed. It's a fact that poor performance means being sent down to the minors, especially for those players who are not established Major League players. It is also difficult to deal with having very little control over my own success. An agent's success is based on their player's success. In most careers, hard work pays off. But there are no guarantees in sports, especially with injuries. And no matter how hard a player tries to stay healthy, every pitcher can potentially get injured each time he throws the ball.

There were some baseball seasons when I was relieved when the season was over. The constant stress of the players' performances was challenging, and knowing most of my players were one bad outing from getting sent back down to the minors. It was certainly difficult for the player as well, and I was usually the first person he called when he got sent down. I would see his name on caller ID, and inevitably know why he was calling. But I would always take the call, no matter the time of day.

There is also the constant threat of losing a player to other agencies. The further my players moved up, the more the other agencies tried to lure them away from me. Some agencies wouldn't hesitate to make promises they couldn't keep. One player left me because an agency promised him a big endorsement deal. I don't know if he ever got the deal, but I do know he only pitched nine games in the Majors. So I didn't lose much, other than some hurt feelings.

Some players also had the mistaken impression that it's the agent who gets them to the Majors. They envisioned me calling the GM, and magically getting them promoted. Certainly, agents advocate for their players, but even Scott Boras, the most powerful and successful baseball agent, doesn't have that kind of power. One of my most loyal players left me because he felt I didn't do enough for him to get to the Majors. Another agent told me the player had said I was like a brother to him. So much for loyalty.

At the end of 2010, Taylor started to feel better, both physically and mentally, but rumor said he was damaged goods. Every team I talked to had questions. I obtained Taylor's medical records while I was at the Winter Meetings and, with Taylor's permission, I quickly dispersed them to interested teams. I also received a call from Sandy Alderson, the new GM for the Mets. He was the only GM to call me about Taylor. We met in person in the Mets suite, and he expressed interest in Taylor. Although I didn't volunteer any information at the time, I later told Sandy about what happened to Taylor during the previous season.

Several teams were willing to offer Taylor a minor league contract, with enough incentives to equal his previous salary if he made the Majors. All things being equal, Taylor would have signed with the Pirates since it meant he would have been reunited with his former manager with the Rockies, Clint Hurdle. However, Sandy Alderson was willing to take a chance on Taylor, and give him a Major League contract. The only catch was that Taylor would agree to sign for $600,000, and get an additional $400,000 if he made the club. Taylor passed a physical, and was a New York Met.

Taylor had a 0.00 ERA during spring training and, after assuring Sandy Alderson Taylor was okay, he made the club and earned an additional $400,000. Aaron Laffey was also in the Majors with the Seattle Mariners, as he was traded during spring training. Aaron was also in the bullpen, although it wasn't his preference. Both Taylor and Aaron started out well, Taylor with a 1.32 ERA, and Aaron with a 1.80 ERA during the month of April. I was able to see Aaron pitch in Baltimore, and Taylor in Washington. Things were going well.

Toward the end of May, things changed again. Taylor gave up runs in consecutive outings, and he called me right after Jon's high school graduation ceremony. He told me his arm hurt, and the anxiety was back. He had to shut it down. I called Sandy Alderson immediately, and Taylor met with him. Sandy told Taylor he could take as much time off as he needed. Both Taylor and I were pleasantly surprised at how Sandy handled the situation. Taylor was placed on the disabled list, and would not pitch again all season.[12]

Aaron Laffey would stay in the Majors for all but 10 days. He had done well through the all-star break but, when he began giving up runs, he was optioned by the Mariners, and then designated for assignment to make room for another player they needed to add to their 40-man roster. The Yankees claimed Aaron, and he finished the season with them. The Yankees designated Aaron at the end of the season, but he was claimed again, this time by the Royals. Ironically, the GM was with the Braves when Aaron was drafted, so we figured the Royals would tender him since Aaron was finally arbitration eligible, having missed arbitration by seven days the previous season with the Indians.

The Royals called prior to the tender date to make an offer. It was certainly not a good sign, and it wasn't even a good offer. Since the Royals saw Aaron only as a reliever, and Aaron wanted to be a starter, it was an easy decision to reject the offer. Aaron was eventually non-tendered, and signed a minor league deal with the Blue Jays, who specifically said they saw Aaron as a starter.

But the chances of enough income from baseball for the 2012 season weren't looking good. Taylor had decided to take the year off and get away from the game, hoping to get his desire for the game, and his health, back. But true to his character, Taylor and his wife shared his decision with me personally, as they drove from his home near Philadelphia to mine in Maryland.

---

[12] Taylor shared his story. In 2012, in an article appeared in the NY Daily News titled *Former NY Mets pitcher Taylor Buchholz stares down his depression.*

> *6/8/11*
>
> *Taylor wanted to let me know how badly he feels about not being able to make me a lot of money. He's an awesome person – considers me part of his family – says I've done a lot more for him than I know. Felt good about our meeting, and I did share the Bible with him – A message of hope.*

Taylor didn't use the word retirement, so he left open the possibility of coming back in 2013. But I knew that, in addition to his mental health, he had found out he had a torn labrum, which meant he needed to get his arm healthy.

Aaron Laffey had 16 starts for Toronto in 2012 and, since he was earning an $800,000 salary while he was in the Majors, I managed to earn $15,000 in fees. But no team offered him a Major League contract in 2013. He signed with the Mets, and was up in the Majors for the month of April in the 2013 season. After being sent down to the minors at the end of April, he never made it back up again (except for a week with the Rockies in 2015).

Of the three players drafted in the 5th round of the 2008 draft, only one of them, Pete Andrelcyzk, made it past A ball. He topped out at AAA, but never made it to the Majors.

By 2013, working as a baseball agent was becoming a hobby. My baseball revenue was minimal. My son, Michael, described it best – I was a full-time lawyer and a part-time baseball agent.

> *7/21/13*
>
> *Still struggling with God's direction with baseball – I'm not making any money. Heard a sermon on the radio – we make plans, but God directs our path. Don't know if God is directing with baseball – watching Ian do poorly; Pete telling me his arms hurt a little, and Aaron's struggles has me wondering. The doors continue to close with baseball. The doors are opening with law cases – lots of new money coming in.*

I'd heard a sermon on the radio that referred to Proverbs 16:9, the same verse I had written in my journal back in 1995. It went along with the advice to paddle and let God steer.

I had already accepted that I couldn't be both a successful baseball agent and a successful lawyer at the same time. But I still had a commitment to pay back the investors through 2015, so I felt obligated to hold on. However, my time was primarily spent rebranding myself as a lawyer. I was rebuilding my client base, and slowly making progress with each passing year. By 2016, I was finally fully supporting my family with the law practice.

Although the work could be a grind, especially with the increase of the family law practice, I continued to find ways to serve God with my skills. I volunteered once a month at a legal clinic with the Good Samaritan Advocates. The leader, Chip Grange, asked if I would co-lead a clinic at the jail. This began a monthly commitment with another attorney, Claude Allen, until COVID came in 2020.

I was also asked to lead the mission trip to West Virginia with our church in 2013 and, although I didn't have any construction skills, I realized God had given me leadership skills. So that became a yearly commitment from

2013 to 2015, and it helped me transition to new things after letting go of my dream.

However, God had not completely closed the door to representing baseball players. Back in 2009, I had taken a chance on Ian Thomas, a pitcher at VCU (Virginia Commonwealth University) who wasn't drafted. A friend of his family contacted me after the 2009 draft, and asked if I could help him get a job. Since he was a left-handed pitcher, I said yes. About a week later, I received a call from a coach with an independent ball team, looking for a left-handed pitcher! The timing couldn't have been better. Still, it would take another three years of independent ball before Ian would get noticed by the Braves. They started him out in Low A ball. The next year he was in AA, and he was invited to Major League spring training in 2014.

He said he was planning on making the team, and he did just that. There I was again, at a Major League game for the debut of one of my players for the 4th time, and it was for a player who was never drafted. I was pleasantly surprised, and it felt like God was rewarding me for my obedience to Him. This time it was opening day of the 2014 season for the Nationals, 40 minutes from my home. Most everyone there was going as a fan. I was going as Ian Thomas's agent. Ian pitched in a total of 30 games over a two-year period, with the Braves in 2014, and the Dodgers in 2015. That would be the last time I had a player in the Majors.

With Ian Thomas, Spring Training 2016

From 2016 to 2022, I represented minor league players, but I was back to being a full-time lawyer. I still had one or two local players in the draft up through 2018, and I didn't want to abandon the players I represented. The last player I represented in affiliated ball was David Ellingson, a 33rd round draft pick in 2016 from Georgetown University. He made it to AA in 2022, but that proved to be his undoing, and he retired at the end of the season.

Incidentally, I had been contemplating running for office, and had some journal entries about it dating back to 1997. In 2018, I felt God leading me to run for the House of Delegates in Maryland. Although I lost the election, it was another reminder that it's better to be obedient than to have earthly success, and that I'm a risk taker. I'm always up for a challenge and an adventure.

I continued to represent my players until one by one they were released. By the end of 2022, I considered myself officially retired from being a sports agent. It became clear I had to move on from representing players, and I was OK with that. I had continued to grow in my faith, and become more open to God's leading. My life was better because of the risk I'd taken, and I was relieved I wouldn't look back on my life and have regrets.

CHAPTER 22

Living with Purpose

> The purpose of life is not to be happy. It is to be useful, to be honorable, to be compassionate, to have it make some difference that you have lived and lived well.
>
> — RALPH WALDO EMERSON

As I became more and more at peace with returning to full-time law practice, and letting go of my baseball agency, I saw God grow and prosper my work in unexpected ways. Recently, I was given an amazing opportunity to take over the law practice of an established estate planning lawyer who was retiring. Even more significant than revamping my own practice, God led me to working part-time with Christian Legal Aid of DC, a place where help is provided to those who can't afford a lawyer.

As for my good friend and former partner, Joe Kohm, he got out of the baseball agent business before I did, and went in a completely different direction. He was ordained as an Anglican priest in 2021, and assigned to a church in Virginia Beach where he lives with his wife. When I emailed him in 2023, and told him I was officially no longer a baseball agent since my last remaining player had retired, he responded:

Wow, Dave – the end of an era... You did so many good things as an agent. I think it's great you are serving those who really need it with your legal skills. You are a great lawyer. Just the fact that we had guys in the big leagues is really amazing... I guess the only thing I miss is the competition of getting players. Just recently I started watching baseball again, and enjoying it as a fan. It is a great game. I was very fortunate to have you for a partner.

With Joe Kohm, September 2023 in Virginia Beach

As for the players I represented, many are married and have families of their own. I stay in touch with a few of them through Christmas cards and Facebook. My hope is that I had a positive influence on them so that they have purpose in their lives beyond baseball.

On the home front, my three boys developed into young men. Looking at them all now, grown young adults, I can't help but wonder how my passion to be a sports' agent impacted them. As it turns out, each of them has pursued their own dreams and adventures, including overseas experiences.

They have landed in different – and challenging – careers in education, engineering, and the military (bomb disposal). I couldn't be prouder of my sons.

Jon (31), Sam (25) and Michael (29)
May 23, 2025

I have been married to Marie now for 33 years, and we have learned a lot about how two people, with very different personalities, can accept each other and work out our differences. As I look back on the risks I took to be a sports' agent, and what that choice meant for Marie, I am extremely grateful. It was my dream, but it was our life. Marie chose to adjust some of her dreams to allow me to pursue mine.

I'm thankful for the ways it taught us to grow together. Marie identifies herself as an extremely cautious person ... but she would attest that she is learning to take risks, even in the face of uncertainty. I, on the other hand, am learning to slow my pace when needed, and be more collaborative in decision-making.

The struggles we had in our marriage have given us a desire to help others, and to share some of the things we have learned. Shifting away from the baseball business allowed us to refocus on new goals. For example, Marie and I have worked together as a team to lead classes on marriage at our church, using our own first-hand experience in resolving conflict, and finding compromise. We have the kind of marriage that's very different from the one I saw growing up, and I'm thankful, all those years ago, when I chose her to be my wife.

When I think back to the day in 1995 when I sat with Frank Young, and he advised me to start paddling and pray, and God will steer, I have been following this advice throughout my career. Sometimes, I've been doing the steering ... and I continue to learn to surrender my ambitions to God, and listen to His leading. At times I've had to learn the hard way. But I've come to believe it can be God's will to be a baseball agent, or a lawyer, and or any other career, providing we are living out our faith in whatever we do. Colossians 3:17 says: 'And whatever you do, whether in word or deed, do it all in the name of the Lord Jesus, giving thanks to God the Father through Him.'

In 1995, when my father shared his regrets just before he died, it made me consider my life dreams, and take big risks. Many years later, after taking the leap, I am grateful for the opportunity to pursue a dream ... and make choices my dad didn't have the opportunity to make. Plus, thanks to the experience, I shared incredible moments with my wife and the boys. I treasure the memories, captured in photos of my son, Michael, in front of every Major League stadium we went to together – a total of eight stadiums. I'll always cherish the joy on Jon's face when we discovered new skate parks on our baseball trips, and seeing Sammy light up when he got to join his older brothers, and I, at a game. So, in this lens, it was a success. A major one.

But even more importantly, I discovered more about how to surrender to God and allow Him to lead me ... and how I often learned more through our failures than successes. Although God provided some wins as a baseball agent, through players who got signed and earned income, He ultimately brought me back to the law practice where I could make good use of my skills ... and I accepted that.

Today you can still find me at the baseball field, but now as a player in the Ponce De Leon Senior Baseball league in the Washington DC area (old man's baseball). Playing on a baseball team has brought me back to my lifelong love of the game – including the challenge, comradery, and competition of sports.

There is also a sense of freedom and joy that I have when I get out on that field, to feel the leather glove in my hand, and to hear the crack of a bat. I can set aside all the things I can't control, and focus on what I <u>can</u> do – which is to play my heart out and, at age 65, I can still run well! It's what helped me stay sane, and have moments of joy in my tumultuous childhood. It also connects me to my dad whom, I believe, experienced moments of joy – to override the disappointment he felt about his life – as he cheered me on during my little league games. Whether we won or lost, Dad always had a big smile, and an affirming pat on the back after the game.

Batting in the Ponce De Leon Baseball League

What do I want life to be like when I look back at the end of my life? Will I regret any roads not taken? It's the question I asked myself years ago, and the answer led me toward this dream of becoming a baseball agent. As I continue to ask myself this question today, I now look at my life more from a spiritual perspective. And, hopefully, at the end of my life I will say that I have fought the good fight, I have finished the race, I have kept the faith (2 Timothy 4:7).

As I reflect on the risks I took to pursue my dream, I realize now that the risk that has, by far, made the biggest difference in my life, is the risk to surrender my life and decisions to God – and to pursue and follow Him and His purposes. And my desire is for God to lead me into the next chapters of my life.

Dedication

Dedicated to my dad who never knew how much of a difference he made to all those who had the privilege to know him.

Acknowledgements

First and foremost, I thank God who took me through this journey.

To my wife, Marie, who went along this journey with me, and sacrificed her dreams so I could pursue mine.

To my sons, Jon, Michael and Sam, who were ready and willing to join me on my travels. So many good memories enjoying time with you.

To Joe Kohm, a great friend, and the best business partner I could have ever hoped for.

To the best editor I know, Danielle Ripley Burgess. Thank you for helping me to find my voice.

To all the players and their families who allowed me to serve as their advisor and agent.

www.ingramcontent.com/pod-product-compliance
Lightning Source LLC
LaVergne TN
LVHW041623070426
835507LV00008B/418